What Is Life All About?

Fred Furrow

Published by Noble Readers Society
Freeport Center
91 E 1700 S
Clearfield, Utah 84015
USA
www.noblereaders.com

© 2025 Fred Furrow
All rights reserved. No part of this publication may be reproduced, distributed, or transmitted in any form or by any means, including photocopying, recording, or other electronic or mechanical methods, without prior written permission of the publisher, except in the case of brief quotations embodied in reviews and certain other noncommercial uses permitted by copyright law.

Paperback ISBN: 979-8-9939118-0-9
Hardcover ISBN: 979-8-9939118-1-6
eBook ISBN: 979-8-9939118-2-3

LCCN: 2025925226

Cover and interior design: Noble Readers Society
Printed in the United States of America

Contents

INTRODUCTION 5

1   Learning the Basics 7

2   The Love Factor The Basic of the Basics 13

3   The Joy of Giving to Others 35

4   Challenges in Life! 45

5   What Is Your "Why"? 59

6   Developing Your Character for God's Plan 73

7   Be There for Others! 93

8   Learn to Do All the Little Things Well! 101

9   What Are You Worrying About? 107

10   Is Your Job Your "Why"? A Plan to Move Forward 113

ENDORSEMENTS 121

FRED FURROW RECOGNIZED
FOR ENTREPRENEURIAL SUCCESS 123

INTRODUCTION

What is life all about? Do we really have a destiny and a purpose for being here? What is your purpose in life? How do you know what your destiny in life is, and will you recognize it?

These are all questions most of us ask ourselves at one time or another. They are good questions. "What is life is all about?" Together we will look to possibly find out what life is all about for you through the experiences of the author and his perspective on life!

I felt that I needed to write this book to share how I learned that God had an incredible plan for my life, but I did not realize it until I was fifty years of age. You might be at a time in your life wondering why you are here and what life is all about. Does God have a plan for you?

What are you doing in your life? The following thoughts and experiences are outlined in a way that no matter what your calling in life is, no matter what your dream or what you desire to do in your life will provide benefit to live a more fulfilled life with joy, happiness, and an understanding of what life is really all about. We will explore how to get back to what I call God's basics. Learn the basics and start to dream!

Are you frustrated with life because nothing ever seems to work out for you? I have learned that most people are living their life unhappy and feel like they are just putting in their time. They are not sure why they are here. They are not happy in their job or at home. When you look at how wonderful life is, why is it that so many people are so unhappy?

I would like to share with you my thoughts and experiences of what life is all about. I would hope that you will find some truths about life and how you can become a better you to reach an understanding of your "why" in life.

1

Learning the Basics

The famous football coach Lou Holtz once said there are four things to remember about life: "Always have something to do, always have someone to love, always have something to hope for, and always have something to believe in."

Let's take a look at "Always have something to do." What does this mean? Does it apply to your occupation, or just doing something? I would like to discuss this "Always have something to do" in the terms of your vocation and why you are here on earth. What is the purpose of your life? Do you realize that most people are going through the motions of life?

They are not sure why they are here, or what they are supposed to do. This might be you. If this is you, then I dedicate this book to you. You should know that your purpose in life may not be related to your chosen occupation. Many times it may be, but for many their true purpose for a happy fruitful life is not related to what they do for a living, but is related to their character and their relationships with family and other people.

Together, we are going to explore why you are here, what life is all about, and how you will know you are on the right path.

> Trust in the Lord with all your heart, and lean not on your own understanding. In all your ways acknowledge Him, and He shall make your paths straight. (Prov. 3:5–6)

God has a plan for your life. You were not born to just eat, take up space, grow old, and die. You will want to learn what I call God's basics in how to treat people in developing your life character. You will learn how God has a plan for your life to give to others. When we talk about giving to others, I do not just mean giving of your money, but giving of your time to serve others. Giving of your love, your understanding, your compassion toward others. We all need to make a living. We are taught from a young age to go to school and get good grades and graduate so you can get a good job so you can support your family. Have a long career so you can have good benefits and retire. Is that what life is all about?

Most people today are on that path! What is a good job? Is it the pay that makes a good job? Is it the benefits that make a good job? Is it the location that makes a good job? Is it doing something you like that makes it a good job? What is a good job?

We will be talking about jobs and the impact they have on your life, both good and bad, later. But right now, I need to ask you a question! If you die tomorrow, how many people would come to your funeral, and why would they come?

Would they come because they are immediate family? Would family living long distances make the special effort to come to your funeral? How many business associates would attend? How many friends would come? Would you have ten people show up? One hundred, five hundred, one thousand-plus? What is your legacy, and would the celebration of your life be a celebration for all the lives you had an impact on?

I have often thought of this question as I have attended funerals where there were less than twenty or so people, and then I have attended funerals where there were several thousand. Why such a difference? It is my discovery that the main difference is how that person made a difference to others during their life. How they impacted other lives! How they treated other people! How they got involved with people through organizations, whether that be their church, service clubs, the PTA, or other service organizations. How they cared for other people! How they loved other people! How many people live their life to impact others in a positive way? These are God's basics in life. Taking the time to learn God's basics is the first step in understanding God's plan for you and your purpose.

It is my hope that you will discover from reading this book that the life God has given you is truly wonderful, and that you will want to live that life every day in a loving, caring, and giving way. By putting God's basics into practice you will develop a kind, warm and joyous love of people and of life!

If we assume that if you were born for a purpose and that God has a plan for your life, then why do so many people get so sidetracked and are not living God's plan?

Most of us do not understand, and I must admit for much of my life I did not understand that God had a plan for my life I thought, like most of us, that my life is up to me. What I make of my life is all on me. I became a true believer of self-help books. Develop a positive attitude! Be enthusiastic and work hard. I wanted to become successful, which in my mind meant to make a lot of money so I could enjoy the good life with my family. I was no different than most people. I had big goals and wanted to be successful. I developed an entrepreneur attitude, which in my mind meant I wanted to control my own destiny and not work for someone else.

I had a mother in my life that had a very positive influence on me. She was always encouraging me in whatever I had decided to do.

So as a senior in college, I knew exactly what I wanted to do to start my own business. I wanted to start my own travel agency in my hometown of Santa Maria, California. So immediately after graduating from Fresno State, I moved back to Santa Maria and started Recreation and Travel Enterprise Inc.

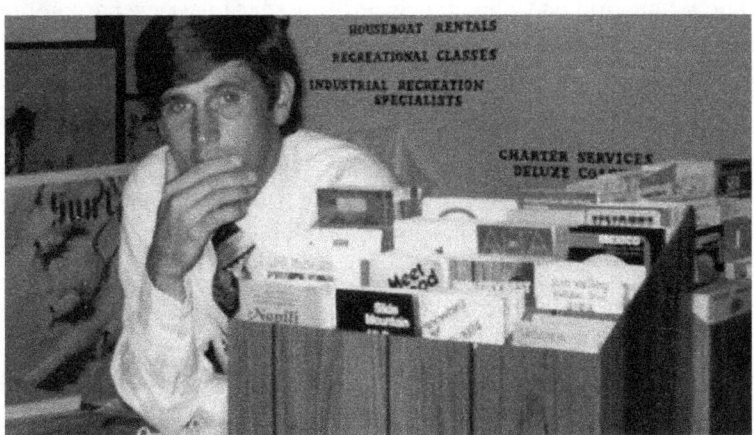

I raised some start-up money from family and friends and took on an equal partner who I graduated from high school with.

As I look back on this experience, which ended in a legal battle with my partner, I think about the experiences that I have had in starting the ten companies that I have been involved in. Since graduating from college, I now see why I failed with several and had moderate success in others. I realized that everything that I did was a learning experience for what God truly had in mind for his plan for my life. Oh, do not get me wrong; each of the companies that I started I thought was going to be the big one. I do not think anyone starts a new business with the attitude "Well, if I fail, it will be a good lesson." No, you start with every intention of making it. I now understand that the hard learning lessons were all part of God's plan for me. Without those lessons, I would not have developed the knowledge and the wisdom I would need for his ultimate plan for my life. Starting a new company is a very hard thing to do. You need to raise the proper capital for operation until the company generates a positive cash flow, and that is always a problem. You need to have good personnel and have a strong business and marketing plan, which are all essential for success.

If you have ever started a business, you know what I am talking

about. It is a frightening proposition to say the least. Yet it is such an exciting experience as well.

As I started each company, I thought at that time that it was going to be the one company that I would develop to be my career. Looking back over the last fifty years, I have had a wonderful journey. The ups and downs, the successes and the failures all provided such a joy with such great memories and so many fantastic relationships.

I know that God had a hand in everything that I have ever accomplished. He opened doors, and he closed doors. He wanted me to experience not only success but also failure. He humbled me when I thought it was all about me.

Where are you in your life right now? Have you had some failures? How have the failures affected you and your personality? Are you bitter? Do you hold a grudge against someone? Are you blaming someone or something for your failure? If that is the case, you need an attitude checkup. You need to celebrate those failures. In fact, you need to get more excited about those failures no matter how little or large they may have been. Yes, get excited! Why? Because they were just learning experiences to make you wiser in your decision-making in the future. What I have come to realize is that God does have a plan for my life. He has a plan for your life. He loves you. He created you for a purpose. Once you realize that and you accept that with hope and faith, you will not believe how your life will change. It is a matter of accepting the truth about you and your relationship with God.

Oh, you can do it your way, but why would you want to? God has a plan for you, that is probably ten times more magnificent than what you can envision for yourself. As I look at my life and what God has done, wow, it is hard to believe that the plan that God had for me was so much larger than my largest dream. I want to tell you I am big dreamer. I have always been a big dreamer, but there is no way I could outdream GOD.

Doesn't it make sense to have God on your side? Have God as your coach! Have God as your mentor! Have God as your partner and best friend! Who could be a better mentor than the All-Knowing God who created you and knows every hair on your head?

Many people, once they experience that first failure, let their dreams die with that failure. They take the attitude "what's the use? I will probably just fail again anyway." Others are so afraid of failing, they never even try. They are influenced by a relative or friend. "Boy, that sounds pretty risky to me." "What makes you think you can do that?" "You're not good enough to do that." Whether it is a parent, family member or a good friend who we are influenced by, they give up on their dream.

Going back to the assumption that you were born for a purpose and God has a plan for you, how do you get on the right path? Well, in these chapters, we are going to talk about what I believe are God's basics. When you learn these basics, everything else will then fall into place. You will discover the life that God has planned for you.

Most coaches in sports teach that when you master the basics, the advanced skills will naturally follow. Stick to the basics. I believe that God has outlined some basics in how you are to live your life.

In searching for your purpose in life, God really wants you to learn those basics.

So, over the next few chapters, we are going to discuss what I refer to as God's basics. I believe that so many of us today are lost. We have no clue as to what life is all about. We have no clue as to what God's plan for our life is. If you are feeling this way, I hope that this work will help you to discover how wonderful life is. You then will understand that God does have a plan for you. If you start to look for that plan, he will lead you to that plan and then lead you through it. Once you have this understanding, the joy of life will overwhelm you. Your attitude for the love of life will be so great you will not know how to express it.

You might be thinking, *Yeah, right. If God had such a great plan for my life, why am I so miserable, discouraged, angry, and confused about my life?* Who have you been listening to? Have you stopped dreaming for some reason? God gives us the right to make choices in our life. He gives us free will, and we choose who we should listen to and associate with.

If you are feeling that your life is a failure and you are not happy in life, you have probably been trying to do everything your way. You have been trying to work your own plan for your life. If you are serious about wanting to make a change in your life to find your purpose, to experience unparalleled happiness, then you need to make the decision that you are tired of doing it your way. You need to accept the fact that before you were born, God had a plan for your life. His plan is of great purpose for you while here on Earth. During the time you spend reading this book, I hope that God will reveal himself to you. If you will make this commitment of understanding, then I would hope that you would want to accept Jesus Christ as your savior. Ask him to come into your life to set you free. This is the first key to you finding your why. Once you have accepted Jesus Christ, then you need to understand that God has developed what I call the basics of living your life. When I came to accept Jesus Christ as my savior, my whole attitude toward life changed. I had such a burden lifted off my shoulders. I could not explain it. I felt alive and had a joy that was so exciting about being alive.

As you look to find God's plan for your life, you will discover that he has the most unbelievable road map to follow. You will find this road map in his teachings and in his word. So, let's explore some of the basics.

2

The Love Factor
The Basic of the Basics

Do you love people? Do you have a loving, caring attitude toward people? Not just for your family, but also for people! Start your new life tomorrow by loving people and having a true attitude of caring for others. Developing your love factor is one of God's basics!

When you love people, show a loving, caring attitude toward them in such a way that they feel your love. When they know that your love is true in spirit, then I believe you will have the first understanding of what life is all about. Not only will you make someone feel good, but you will also have that wonderful feeling of making a difference in someone's life.

People will want to associate with you! They will trust you and will want to be your friend when they sense you care. People know when someone has the love factor coming from their heart.

> Don't just pretend to love others. Really love them. Hate what is wrong. Hold tightly to what is good. Love each other with genuine affection, and take delight in honoring each other. Never be lazy, but work hard and serve the Lord enthusiastically. Rejoice in our confident hope. Be patient in trouble and keep on praying. When God's people are in need, be ready to help them. Always be eager to

practice hospitality. (Rom. 12:9–13 NLT)

God put you here to make a difference. Making a difference comes in the way of a smile, a loving, caring touch, in your tone of voice, your positive facial expressions. Being a giver by just giving of some of your time in a loving way or just listening. These are all in themselves little things but together express that you have a loving spirit that lets people know that you care and everyone you meet will know that you have it. You have the love factor.

> "That Christ may dwell in your hearts by faith; that ye, being rooted and grounded in love" (Eph. 3:17 KJV).

In Galatians 5:22, "But the Holy Spirit produces this kind of fruit in our lives: love, joy, peace, patience, kindness, goodness, faithfulness, gentleness, and self-control. There is no law against these things!"

This scripture outlines the nine love factor basics from God. If you allow God to come into your heart, the Holy Spirit will go to work on the developing your love factor. You can see that love is the first fruit of the Spirit. The other eight fruits of the love factor all contribute to you finding the plan that God has for your life.

There are so many things that you can say about love. You need to know if you are not happy in your personal relationships or your work relationships, then you are probably not applying the "love factor" to what you do and the relationships you have.

God wants you to have your life based on a strong foundation. Love is the one factor that will stabilize your life on a strong foundation like anchoring down to bedrock. As you weather storms in your life, you will want to embed your life into the rock of love. Just as you would put the foundations of your home into rock so your home will not be blown away or eroded away by a storm. If your foundation for your life is love, then like your home, your life will not be washed away or eroded by the many storms you will face in your life. That is why I believe developing the love factor in your life is one of God's most important basics.

What Is the Love Factor?

There are so many elements that contribute to the love factor in your life. Some are more obvious than others, but believe me, all are so very important

WHAT'S LIFE ALL ABOUT?

in understanding what life is all about. God loves you and wants you to love him and everyone you meet.

> "And let us consider one another to provoke
> unto love and to good works" (Heb. 10:24 KJV).

Developing a loving Spirit takes some practice. You need to know that sometimes it takes a concentrated awareness of what you are saying, doing, and how you are acting will together play a very important part in developing a loving spirit. I always loved the expression "Do unto others.as you would have them do unto you."

How do I develop a loving spirit?

> "Let everything you do be done in love (true
> love to God and man as inspired by God's love for
> us)" (1 Cor. 16:14).

Love Yourself

You first need to understand the power of loving God and loving yourself. It is so hard to love others and develop the loving spirit if you do not love yourself. This is such a large subject, and there have been so many books written on this subject and I would recommend that if you do not have a wonderful love for life and know that you truly love yourself that you need to look in the mirror and ask yourself, "Do I love the person that I am looking at in the mirror?" If you do not know the answer or if you do not love yourself, I would recommend that you seriously seek counseling.

> "And this I pray, that your love may abound yet
> more and more in knowledge and in all judgment"
> (Phil. 1:9 KJV).

The Magic of a Loving Smile
A Key Component of the Love Factor

The first thing that you can do in developing yourself into a loving spirit is to smile. Yes, smile all the time. Smile at everyone you meet. Put a smile in your voice. Have you ever been talking to someone on the phone that just had a smile in their voice?

It was like they came through the phone and put a caring hand on your shoulder, and their voice just had a smile that said "I care about you. I want to help you. I love people and life, and whatever I can do to help you this day, I want to do that." They had a *smile in their voice*. So, start to put a smile in your voice.

Do you know when you are smiling, it is very hard to think or act in a negative way. A smile is a gesture of love, and if you are smiling, you will be giving off caring, loving vibrations to those around you. People will want to be around you because you will light up any room you enter. People are very intuitive about how others give off vibrations. Your smile may be the only loving thing given to someone in their whole day. So, smile. You need to practice it. People who are not used to seeing you smile will be asking you, "What are you smiling about?" You need to be prepared with positive loving answers. "I am smiling because I am so glad to see you." "Seeing you just makes my whole day bright." "I am smiling because I am so happy, and I just love life and am so grateful that you are a part of my life." Or you may start a little slower so people who know you do not think you have gone over the edge. So then you just say, "I just feel really happy today and cannot help but smile." Or "It's just a great day and just makes me want to smile." You need to be you but make the change of smiling at everyone every day. People might be a little shocked at first, especially if you were a person without a loving spirit before, but keep working on developing your loving spirit. You will see your family and friends and people you work with respond to your loving spirit in a very loving positive way. They will want to be around you because your loving spirit will make them feel good. You will be touching their lives, making an impact.

Making the effort to smile says so many wonderful things about you. A smile says, "I care." A smile says, "I love you." A smile is very contagious. It is very hard to smile at someone and not have them smile back. Try it.

Smile with a joyful heart. Smile at strangers. Smile at the teller in the bank. Smile at the clerk at the grocery store. As you are smiling, say a kind word or a kind greeting.

"Hi, Sally, I hope you are having a wonderful day!" How did you know her name was Sally? Almost all grocery stores, bank tellers, people in service and retail wear name tags.

Every time I opened an account with a new bank for business or a personal account, I would make a point to introduce myself to the manager, the assistant manager, and the service manager. I learned their names and asked for all their business cards. Every time that I entered that bank, I

WHAT'S LIFE ALL ABOUT?

would make a point to notice who was in the bank and I gave them a "smile." A warm greeting, calling them by their name says, "I care about you." Each time I would go to a new teller, I would call them by their name (from their name tags), and I give them a warm greeting. You can say something like "Ann, hope you are having a great day." What happens over a few weeks or months? Let me tell you. Everyone in the bank ends up learning your name as you continue to address the tellers with a warm smile and greeting and call them by their name. They make a point to learn your name by looking at your banking transaction. As you enter the bank with your signature smile, and they will start give returning your smile and are say hello. How many times have I heard, "Hello, Fred, how are you today, and how can I help you?" Soon you will have made friends with most of the bank employees. After time goes by, you ask questions to engage them in conversation, showing that you care about them. You ask them a question about their family, their children, their grandchildren, about their day, and then listen. Many times, they will tell you their whole life story. You are being a good friend by being a good listener. Do this wherever you go and wherever you do business. Wouldn't it give you a good feeling if everyone you did business with knew your name and you knew theirs? And if they greeted you with a smile and by calling you by your name? Everyone loves to hear their name, and the fact that you made the effort to learn their name is one of the basics of developing the love factor and the loving spirit. *It is what life is all about!*

> "Now these three remain: faith, hope, and love.
> But the greatest of these is love" (1 Cor. 13:13).

A lesson learned.

I must tell you the story of my youngest son Scott. In his senior year of high school, they opened a new Vons grocery store close to our home. He applied as a box boy and was hired right away. Scott is somewhat shy when it comes to talking to people that he does not know. So, my advice to Scott was, "Son, what you need to do is smile and ask people questions about themselves. Get to know people, and they will want to know you." I told him to ask his management questions like "How long you have been with Vons?" Then just listen. When they stop talking, ask them another question about their family and then just listen. So many people just want someone to show an interest in them. By asking questions and then listening, you have shown a true interest in that person. You have started a friendship, a relationship, a caring attitude about other people.

The result was that Scott came home one day and said, "Dad, you were so right. I asked my managers questions like you suggested, and they ended up telling me their whole life story."

Scott was promoted in just three weeks to a clerk and then in a couple of months into produce, and then handling the dairy department. He took a caring attitude to make friends with those he worked with and serviced as customers. His smile and loving attitude were recognized and rewarded in a very short time. Scott worked at Vons for about one and half years and has not worked there for over fifteen years now, but every time that I am in that Vons, management ask me about Scott! "How is Scott doing? We sure miss him and wished he was still at the store!"

Our son Scott and his wife Nicole

It starts with a warm sincere smile! Followed by a caring attitude that reflects, "Hey, I would like to know you better, tell me about your family." *Then listen...* Listen with an interest and with the same caring attitude in your smile. Do not ask questions and then have your mind wander and not hear what they are telling you. Take the time to really listen with that caring attitude. You will have an impact on that person and probably have a friend for life. *That is what life is all about!*

My wife Mary and I are so very proud of all five of our boys, because all of them have made it a point to become loving and caring individuals that touch lives wherever they go in life.

Our son Eric was the manager of a jewelry store in Redding, California, and one time, we were visiting and went right to the store in the mall to see him. He was on his lunch break. We decided to wait for him in the store as he was expected back shortly. A very attractive lady in her late fifties entered the store and asked for Eric. The sales staff told her that Eric was on his lunch break and if there was anything he could do for her. She said, "No, I will come back when Eric is here." It turns out this lady was the president of the Chamber of Commerce; she was a very successful businesswoman, and one day in the mall, Eric saw this businesswoman and stepped out of his store to start a conversation. The result of this conversation is that this businesswoman became a very loyal customer. She would only have Eric wait on her, and she spent several thousand dollars every month or so. Eric simply started a conversation with a smile that led to a friendship that led to a very loyal customer. Smile and say hello.

Mary and our son Eric

A very similar situation happened in the sporting goods store where our son Brian was an assistant manager. My wife and I were on that side of town one day and decided to stop in to say hello to Brian, but he was on his lunch break. A boy, about nine years of age, came into the store with his mother and asked one of the sales staff if Brian was working. He was told that he was on his lunch break. The boy very loudly told his mother, "Mom, we have to come back. Brian is not here." It turned out that Brian had made a friend by having a caring attitude in serving this family with their skiing equipment.

Two years later, Brian was employed as the marketing director for our local ski resort, China Peak. He was on his snowboard coming down the mountain, and noticed one of the employees that he managed was operating one of the large Snowcat tractors that are used to groom the slopes. Snowcats have tracks that are three feet wide. As Brian came up to give the Snowcat driver some instructions, the driver did not see him and made a very sharp turn and ended up running over our son. Brian sustained some major injuries, including losing the sight in his right eye. Brian thought the incident was over, but word of his injuries got out. A nine-year-old boy and his family that we met two years prior came to the hospital several times to visit Brian. And all the while Brian was in the hospital, he had a constant stream of visitors day and night. He was very appreciative of everyone caring about him, but he did not get much rest while there. He had over 150 visitors come to see him in the hospital. All were people whose lives Brian had touched in a positive way. God had a plan for Brian, and it was not his time to go to heaven.

Our son Brian

My wife is beyond special and has the most loving, caring spirit of anyone I know. We will be in the grocery store, and she will start talking to someone, carrying on a long conversation as if she had just found her long lost friend of ten years talking about kids and life situations. As I would walk up, she would introduce me to them. Later I would ask her, "Where did you know that person from?" Her reply would always be, "I just met them in the store for the first time."

WHAT'S LIFE ALL ABOUT?

My wife Mary and myself

Smile, say hello, care about people, and take an interest in them. Yours may be the only loving spirit they see all day or all week. Make a difference by caring, by smiling, by making a friend.

These small but very important aspects of developing a loving sprit are a part of God's basics for our lives.

What is life all about? Making a positive impact on others, caring about them, and getting involved! Show everyone that you truly have the love factor, for they are God's basics of life.

> "And may the Lord make you to increase and excel and overflow in love for one another and for all people, just as we also do for you" (1 Thess. 3:12).

The Love Factor Must Start in Your Home, with Your Family

As I was growing up, I always knew my parents loved me, but they never expressed it openly by saying "I love you, son." My father passed away at the age of ninety. In the last few years of his life, I told him how much I loved him. It was so hard for him to say those words or to hear me tell him I loved him. He did not know how to react to "I love you." I knew he loved me, but he was never told by his parents that they loved him. Many families just did not talk to their children like that. It was amazing how hard it was for my father and my mother to learn to say, "I love you." For a very long time when I would tell my mother on the phone that I loved her, she would tear up and it was hard for her to get those words out. Today she tells me before we hang up that she loves me and my wife, and she always asks me to give my wife a big hug for her. If you are not raised in a loving family where love is expressed openly, it becomes a challenge to develop the love factor. It becomes awkward. It is not natural for you as it was not natural for my parents. But it is so important. It is what God has planned for your life to love all those you associate with.

> My purpose is that they may be encouraged in heart and united in love, so that they may have the full riches of complete understanding, in order that they may know the mystery of God, namely, Christ, in whom are hidden all the treasures of wisdom and knowledge. (Col. 2:2–3)

Love is such a wonderful thing, and it needs to be expressed on a daily basis. My wife and I have five boys. I have two boys, Brian, thirty-eight, and Scott, thirty-three, from a previous marriage. My wife had three boys from a previous marriage: David, forty-one; Eric, thirty-nine; and Bryan, thirty-six. Our youngest was four and our oldest was twelve when my wife Mary and I came together with our blended five-boy family.

Our five boys love each other and are best friends. They have all had their challenges in life and still have challenges, as that is also what life is all about (which we will explore in a later chapter!). But love for each other will endure all pain and all challenges.

We are so blessed because all of our boys know what love is and express it to us each day or every time we talk on the phone or see each other. From the time the boys were born and especially when they were old enough to talk and when they ever left the house, we would give them a big hug and tell them that we loved them. To this day, that is a ritual, and what we are so proud of is when the boys were going through those challenging teenage years, you know when Mom and Dad suddenly are not too smart, and as teenagers, the kids become all knowing. One of the things that never changed, no matter where we were or no matter who they were with at the time, is that we gave each other a hug and told each other that we love each other.

During the teenage days, you would think they would say "Yuck, Dad. Yuck, Mom, please, don't hug me and tell me you love me in front of my friends." That was not the case; we always hugged and told each other that we loved them. In fact, we believe that many of their friends wished that their own parents would hug them and tell them they loved them. So, whenever our boys had friends with them and were leaving for whatever reason, we not only hugged our boys and told them we loved them, but we hugged their friends and told them that we loved them also. This meant so much to so many of them, and they still come around to get hugs and to hear us say hello and tell them we love them.

I tell my wife every night before we go to sleep that I love her. I make a point to do the same as many times as I can during the day also. You can never tell someone too many times that you love them.

Loving people and applying the loving, caring principles of the love factor will have a tremendous positive effect on your life with your family, with your friends, and especially with your coworkers on the job. Your having a loving spirit will help you to achieve promotions and reach your goals.

Being able to relate to people is one of the most important aspects of your life. The love factor creates a bond between you and the people that come into your life.

> "And so as those who have been chosen of God, holy and beloved, put on a heart of compassion, kindness, humility, gentleness and patience" (Thess. 3:12).

Make it a goal to meet someone new every day. Challenge yourself to start talking to people. It is really very simple once you just decide to do it. How many times do we get on an elevator with strangers, and no one says a word? What a shame, because this is a great opportunity to compliment someone's appearance or to make any friendly statemen. "That sure is a pretty dress on you!" Elevators are a great place to practice because you only have a short time to say anything. If you think you blew it, they will be getting off the elevator and you will probably never see them again. Have fun, make someone's day.

My wife and I belong to a large church, and we have many elderly greeters and ushers. My wife always greets the elderly gentlemen with "Good morning, *young man*." You should see their faces light up and smile. Most of them thank her and say, "I needed that this morning." Most of them look for her so they can greet her, but the greeting that she gives them makes their whole day. Be kind, talk to people, compliment them. Giving a compliment is one of the nicest things you can do. Give a compliment with a smile; be honest and sincere. A compliment that is not given sincerely would be better left unsaid. So be sincere. People will know when you are sincere. It will be portrayed in your tone of voice, in your eyes, and in your smile. They can all sense your sincerity when you extend someone a compliment.

A poem that a good friend sent me over the internet is called "The Dash." You have probably heard of "The Dash." Well, what is so significant in "The Dash" is that it directly communicates what we are talking about: *"What is life all about?"*

"The Dash" was written by Linda Ellis. As described on Linda's website, Linda was:

> ..."resonating in the back of her mind the words from a letter which had been previously routed around the office. It had been written by the wife of an employee who was aware that she was dying. I was so moved by that letter that I saved a copy of it and continue to live by her words.
>
> Regrets? I have a few. Too much worrying! I worried about finding the right husband and having children, being on time, being late and so on. It didn't matter. It all works out and it would have worked out without the worries and the tears. If I would have known, then what I know now! But I did and so do you. We're all going to die. Stop worrying and start *loving and living*."

Stop worrying and start *"loving and living."* Here is "The Dash." I hope it has as much meaning for you as it does for me.

The DASH by Linda Ellis

> I read of a man who stood to speak
> at the funeral of his friend.
> He referred to the dates on her tombstone from
> the beginning…to the end.
>
> He noted that first came the date of her birthand
> spoke of the second with tears,

WHAT'S LIFE ALL ABOUT?

but he said that what mattered most of all
was the dash between those years.

For that dash represents all the time
that she spent alive on earth,
and now only those who loved her
know what that little line is worth.

For it matters not, how much we own;
the cars, the house, the cash.
What matters is how we live and love
and how we spend our dash.

So think about this long and hard,
are there things you'd like to change?
For you never know how much time is left.
(You could be at "dash mid-range.")

If we could just slow down enough
to consider what's true and real,
and always try to understand
the way other people feel.

And…be less quick to anger,
and show appreciation more
and love the people in our lives
like we've never loved before.

If we treat each other with respect
 and more often wear a smile,
remembering that this special dash
might only last a little while

So, when your eulogy is being read
with your life's actions to rehash…
would you be pleased with the things they have to say
about how you spent your dash?

This is a powerful poem and brings into focus what life is all about with respect to God's basics.

How do you treat people? Are you kind? Do you have a loving spirit about you? Most people are going through life in a whirlwind, so concerned about their job that they are missing out on the true beauty of life. Spending most of their thoughts and actions on making a living! The job for many is all-encompassing. So worried about doing well to get that promotion, to please the boss, that they lose focus on who they are and what is important in life.

It is so easy to get into a rut in life. Get up, get ready for work, work all day, come home, flop down in front of the TV, and hear how bad everything is in life from our news of the day. Who murdered who, who robbed who, what terrorist group bombed what city… The news is typically so negative that if we judge our life by it we tend to rationalize and say we don't have it so bad compared to what is going on in the world.

Most people are not happy with what they do for a living. They are spending most of their lives doing something they do not enjoy while earning only a mediocre living. They are missing out on what is the true joy of life because they are so concerned about "work." They overlook their family, their friends, and are not taking moments to just love people and life.

One of my recommendations is for you to implement every morning is to say out loud to yourself or with your spouse four things that you love about life. "I love how the sun wakens each new morning with a ray of hope!" "I love life and I expect to have a fantastic day!" "I love you my husband (or wife) and am so excited knowing the day will bring you great things!" "I love our life and all the blessings the Lord has bestowed on us!" I have found that if you love life, it will love you back and grant you deep happiness, and you will feel like exploding with joy at times.

If you will begin developing God's basics of loving people, caring about people, taking an interest in people, and being a giver, not a taker, you will start to understand the plan that God has for you. You will realize what is important in life, and you will find that you will reset your priorities. This will greatly increase happiness and joy in your life.

> "Love one another with brotherly affection [as members of one family], giving precedence and showing honor to one another" (Rom. 12:10).

WHAT'S LIFE ALL ABOUT?

Breakfast at McDonald's!

This is a story about how one woman amplified the love factor. As you read this story you will see what we are talking about.

The following story is reported to be a true story.

I am a mother of three (ages three, twelve, and fourteen) and have recently completed my college degree. The last class I had to take was Sociology.

The teacher was absolutely inspiring with the qualities that I wish every human being had been graced with.

Her last project of the term was called "Smile."

The class was asked to go out and smile at three people and comment their reactions.

I am a very friendly person and always smile at everyone and say hello anyway. So I thought this would be a piece of cake, literally.

Soon after we were assigned the project, my husband, youngest son, and I went out to McDonald's one crisp March morning.

It was just our way of sharing special playtime with our son.

We were standing in line, waiting to be served, when all of a sudden, everyone around us began to back away, and then even my husband did.

I did not move an inch…an overwhelming feeling of panic welled up inside of me as I turned to see why they had all moved.

As I turned around, I smelled a horrible "dirty body" smell, and there, standing behind me, were two poor homeless men.

As I looked down at the short gentleman close to me, he was "smiling."

His beautiful sky-blue eyes were full of God's light as he searched for acceptance.

He said, "Good day," as he counted the few coins he had been clutching.

The second man fumbled with his hands as he stood behind his friend. I realized the second man was mentally challenged and the blue-eyed gentleman was his salvation.

I held my tears as I stood there with them.

The young lady at the counter asked him what they wanted.

He said, "Coffee is all miss" because that was all they could afford. (If they wanted to sit in the restaurant and warm up, they had to buy something. He just wanted to be warm.)

Then I really felt it—the compulsion was so great I almost reached out and embraced the little man with the blue eyes. That is when I noticed all eyes in the restaurant were set on me, judging my every action.

I smiled and asked the young lady behind the counter to give me two more breakfast meals on a separate tray.

I then walked around the corner to the table that the men and chosen as a resting spot. I put the tray on the table and laid my hand on the blue-eyed gentleman's cold hand.

He looked up at me with tears in his eyes and said, "Thank you."

I leaned over, began to pat his hand, and said, "I did not do this for you. God is here working through me to give you hope."

I started to cry as I walked away to join my husband and son. When I sat down, my husband smiled at me and said, "That is why God gave you to me, honey, to give me hope."

We held hands for a moment, and at that time, we knew that only because of the grace that we had been given were we able to give.

We are not churchgoers, but we are believers.

That day showed me the pure light of God's sweet love.

I returned to college on the last evening of class with this story in hand.

WHAT'S LIFE ALL ABOUT?

> I turned in "my project" and the instructor read it.
>
> Then she looked up at me and said, "Can I share this?"
>
> I slowly nodded as she got the attention of the class.
>
> She began to read, and that is when I knew that we, as human beings and being part of God, share this need to heal people and to be healed.
>
> In my own way, I had touched the people at McDonald's, my son, instructor, and every soul that shared the classroom on the last night I spend as a college student.
>
> I graduated with one of the biggest lessons I would ever learn: "unconditional acceptance."

The important message of this story is to love people! As we come in contact with others not as well off as we have, take the time to show your compassion with a caring, loving heart. Your life will be so much more enriched by continually asking the question. "How can I make a positive difference in someone's life today?" That is the love factor! One of God's basics! *It is what life is all about!*

> "Whereas the object and purpose of our instruction and charge is love, which springs from a pure heart and a good (clear) conscience and sincere (unfeigned) faith" (1 Tim. 1:5).

Many people will walk in and out of your life. True friends will leave footprints in your heart but being a friend even for an instant may impact someone's life in a positive way. Always be on the lookout for the opportunity to make a difference in someone's life.

One of my wife's and my favorite movies is *It's a Wonderful Life*. George Bailey had the opportunity to see what would have happened to his family and the people of Bedford Falls if he had not been born, and thus not been able to prevent tragic events that were destined to occur in the lives of many of them. It really makes you start to think. I hope that my life could have such an impact on others like George Bailey did in his life.

Develop the love factor! If you understand that life is about loving—loving your family, your neighbor, and all who you meet. This is the key to developing the love factor in your life. How can you serve and have your life grow as a person? You will want to learn how to get involved. Get involved with family, people, organizations, people you work with. Be an organizer of fun events. So many times, people would love to get involved, but they do not know how. By being an organizer you provide the opportunity to let people get involved.

I graduated from high school in 1966, and our school was a brand-new school when I was a freshman; and we had juniors, sophomores, and freshman with no seniors that first year. After graduation in June of 1966, I had made a decision to attend all our class reunions. I always had a blast seeing old friends from school and catching up on things that were happening in their lives. After our thirty-year class reunion, the reunion committee was getting burned out as it is a lot of work organizing a reunion. With trying to locate members of the class and making sure they get notified, it does become a grueling task.

So, when it was about a year away from us having our thirtyfifth-year class reunion, none of the past reunion committee was very anxious to even have one. Just too much work! Well, I always had too much fun at our reunions and volunteered to head up the reunion committee to make sure we had our reunion. We decided to invite the class ahead of us in school ('65) and the class behind us ('67). Our class knew many people from these classes and we thought it would be great fun to see them as well. Most of us had not seen these classmates since high school, which was by now thirty-five years. The reunion was a huge success, and everyone just had a blast. I was very fortunate to have a great committee, and we were able to generate a lot of enthusiasm for the reunion. Since we were a new school, we had many of our teachers who were just out of college and were new teachers when the high school opened. We invited about thirty-five of our teachers, and that made it even more special. As part of our program, we had a little teacher roast, which was very well received.

Our committee spent hours and hours on the phone tracking down addresses of classmates. The result of all that effort was that we were able to touch many people's lives the three days of the reunion who might have not come except for the personal contacts we made with them. All the committee members gave many hours of their time. I won't try to thank them all here because that would fill a book in and of itself. But, in most committee situations, you always have one or two people that go way beyond the call of duty in a loving, caring way. Those people for our committee were

WHAT'S LIFE ALL ABOUT?

Jann Williams and her husband Charlie. I knew Charlie in high school since he was in my class. We surfed at a couple of our favorite surf spots, but we were not close friends in high school. Over the years, however, Charlie and Jann have become as close as family. My wife and I love this couple because they would do anything for you. They are the type of friends that if you broke down in the middle of the desert at 1:00 a.m. and called Charlie and Jann, they would say, "We are on our way!" As you go through life, most people hope to develop a close friendship like that with maybe one person. My wife and I are truly blessed as we have developed a close relationship with many great people.

Fred Furrow, Charlie Williams, Mary Furrow, and Jann Williams.

Many of our close friendships are relationships that have been developed by getting involved. Being organizers together! That is how Charlie and Jann have become such close friends. Not only did we have great time at our thirty-fifth class reunion, but we had our fortieth reunion in 2006, and we decided to invite all the classes of the sixties (the classes of 1964, 1965, 1966, 1967, 1968, and 1969) and made it an all-sixties class reunion. It was such fun and the comments that we received back were so fantastic. We had many who had never attended a class reunion and being able to see and talk to fellow classmates after forty years was a wonderful experience. My wife and I received so many thank-you notes and cards; it was fantastic. Seeing everyone have such a wonderful time and be so appreciative makes all the hard work so very worthwhile. We have gone on to have the all-sixties class reunion for our forty-fifth and our fiftieth class reunions. By having the first six classes come together, we have been able to do so much more over a three-day event since over three hundred people participated.

The point that I wanted to make by telling you about our reunion story is that out of the six classes of our school that graduated in the sixties, only one other class has had a regular reunion after their thirty-fifth. It was just too much work to organize. Our class of '66 would have fallen into that mold if it were not for a couple of us who picked up the ball and got involved. We decided it was too important to let go by the wayside. The result is that we had over three hundred attend our last reunion, and we helped to provide a lasting wonderful experience that everyone can hardly wait until we do it again.

Was it a lot of work? Yes, it was, but you know we looked at it as having fun. We had a reunion meeting once a month. My wife and I traveled 150 miles from Fresno, California to Santa Maria, California, but Charlie and Jann traveled from Petaluma to Santa Maria, which was at least an additional three hours more than what we traveled, yet they never missed a meeting. Many on the committee that lived in Santa Maria were only able to make a few of the meetings. We made it fun. We developed long-time friendships, and it all happened because we decided to "get involved." Looking back, all the memories we have of working on the reunions, and of attending the reunions, and the fun of being rewarded by attendees' responses of sincere gratitude for all our hard work made our efforts very much worth it all. Get involved! Being able to express your love factor by having a loving spirit, wanting to make a difference in people's lives can be a part of the plan God has for your life. *It is what life is all about.*

So, if you want to have a fun-filled, rewarding life, and a chance to meet so many new friends, then you need to get involved. Get involved while in school, get involved with clubs, and get involved with service organizations. Get involved with the PTA and get involved with your church. Getting involved engages you with people and life! *It is what life is all about!* And I know it's one of God's basics and a part of the plan that God has for you!

Remember as we live day-to-day, you will want to live each day to the

WHAT'S LIFE ALL ABOUT?

fullest. Never forget that making a difference in people's lives does not depend on your credentials, your degrees, your money, or your awards, but how you care for people and how you apply the love factor to make a difference in people's lives.

3

The Joy of Giving to Others

As you grow in life, in your caring and loving and developing your love factor, you will ultimately learn how important it is to be a giver. Giving is one of the most important things to learn about *what life is all about* and is one of God's basics.

Are you a giver? Being a giver includes so many little things that you do and say. Seek to give of your time in meaningful ways. And when you give your time, do not expect things in return. I do not mean giving time on your job, but giving of your time outside of what you do for a living. Giving time to your family in a nurturing, loving way is where developing a giving spirit needs to start. Giving of your time without expecting anything in return helps you develop a true spirit of giving. What we discussed in chapter 1 regarding the love factor is all part of giving.

> "Since God chose you to be the holy people he loves, you must clothe yourselves with tenderhearted mercy, kindness, humility, gentleness, and patience" (Col. 3:12 NLT).

Does being a giver mean giver of money or gifts? In certain situations it can mean giving of money or gifts, but it really means giving of yourself, giving of your love, and giving of your time. The recipients will know that it comes from your heart. And when you give, give with joy in your heart. Your joy and happiness may infect other with that same joy and happiness. Again, from Galatians 5:22, joy is the second fruit of the Spirit.

> "But the fruit of the Spirit is love, joy, peace, patience, kindness, goodness, faithfulness, gentleness and self-control. Against such things there is no law" (Gal. 5:22–23).

The person that only gives because he or she expects something in return is not truly giving and will not experience the joy of being a giver. The giving we are talking about in *what life is all about* is giving that is done from the heart.

At Thanksgiving and again at Christmas, our small Rotary Club would identify families that needed a Thanksgiving meal, and at Christmas, we would choose a few families and learn about all the members of the family. It was usually a single mother working hard to support several children and struggling to keep the family afloat. I especially enjoyed what we did for families at Christmas. We would learn every family member's name, their ages, and their clothes sizes. Each member of our Rotary Club would go shopping for one of the family members, and we would purchase clothing, toys, and things they really needed, like a warm coat. We would get together and wrap all the presents and label each package with each family member's name. We would also purchase a complete Christmas dinner with turkey, mashed potatoes, dressing, and all the trimmings.

We would deliver these gifts and the Christmas meal to these families and see the tears that would come out in the mother and the children. It made them so very happy. They would cry; we would all cry, and we would get the biggest hug from all the members of the family. It was such a wonderful thing that we were able to do for those families. We gave of our time and our money, but that did not matter. It was giving of our loving spirit through this process that gave all the members of our Rotary such a precious memory. Seeing that single mother and her children so excited and so thankful and so full of love were very special moments that I would not trade for a million dollars.

The time we gave, the money we gave were not ever a consideration. It was the joy of seeing those smiling faces as we arrived at their home bearing gifts of joy, of food, of warmth. You thought that we were the givers, but we soon realized that we received the biggest gift of all. The gift of appreciation and love! Being a giver and not expecting anything in return will always provide you the best gift of all, and the joy it brought to each of our hearts

WHAT'S LIFE ALL ABOUT?

was priceless. Making a difference in someone's life and having a positive influence in making someone happy and bringing them Joy, that is what life is all about!

> "Be kind and compassionate to one another, forgiving each other, just as in Christ God forgave you" (Eph. 4:32).

My boys were always active in elementary school and all through high school. When roller blading was very popular, two of our boys were very good Rollerbladers and even competed in the X games in San Francisco one year. The town where we live, Clovis, California, did not have any place for kids to go to roller-blade. So many of the kids rollerbladed on school sites and at commercial building sites. They were always run off the properties. They were all great kids, just had no place to skate. As a member of our Rotary Club, I had the privilege to serve as its president one year. I had a passion for our club to help raise money for the city to provide a skate park. So over a period of several years, we finally convinced the city to build a very nice skate park with our help. The city named the park the Clovis Rotary Skate Park. The purpose of telling you this story about our skate park is that if you see a need, get involved make things happen. You be the one to take the lead.

Giving for the skate park

Be a part of making a difference in your community.

Have you ever visited a senior home to volunteer to help? To talk to seniors? To give them your time? When you visit a senior home you will find that you will be rewarded with so much kindness that you cannot help but get a warm, fuzzy feeling in your heart. When was the last time you visited your grandparents? When you visit seniors, talk to them, ask them questions about their past. Show a true interest with love. Be a good listener. My grandmother lived to be ninety-eight, and when she was ninety-five, we had her visit us for a week during Christmas. My cousin and I thought it would be a great idea to ask our grandmother questions about her past. So we not only did we ask her questions, but we also secretly recorded the entire conversations for about eight hours over a few days. We asked her about her childhood, about her siblings, about her schooling. She joyously answered each question, telling us all about her life. You could see it was pure pleasure for her to relive her past as she told us her entire life story. But what was even more precious to us is that we had it recorded to share with our children and for us to revisit her life of ninety-eight years whenever we wished.

If you have a grandmother or grandfather, you might think about doing this same thing. It is such a joy for them and a true treasure for you to keep forever.

> But if a widow has children or grandchildren, these should learn first of all to put their religion into practice by caring for their own family and so repaying their parents and grandparents, for this is pleasing to God. (Tim. 5:4)

WHAT'S LIFE ALL ABOUT?

What You Sow, You Shall Reap

My wife sent this in the form of an e-mail one day, and I found that this story is a true goodwill story of *what life is all about*!

What Goes Around Comes Around

The man slowly looked up. This was a woman clearly accustomed to the finer things of life. Her coat was new. She looked like she had never missed a meal in her life. His first thought was that she wanted to make fun of him, like so many others had done before.

"Leave me alone," he growled.

To his amazement, the woman continued standing. She was smiling—her even white teeth displayed in dazzling rows.

"Are you hungry?" she asked.

"No," he answered sarcastically. "I've just come from dining with the president. Now go away." The woman's smile became even broader. Suddenly the man felt a gentle hand under his arm. "What are you doing, lady?" the man asked angrily. "I said to leave me alone."

Just then a policeman came up. "Is there any problem, ma'am?" he asked.

"No problem here, Officer," the woman answered. "I'm just trying to get this man to his feet. Will you help me?"

The officer scratched his head. "That's old Jack. He's been a fixture around here for a couple of years. What do you want with him?"

"See that cafeteria over there?" she asked. "I'm going to get him something to eat and get him out of the cold for a while."

"Are you crazy, lady?" the homeless man resisted. "I don't want to go in there!" Then he felt strong hands grab his other arm and lift him up.

"Let me go, Officer. I didn't do anything." "This

is a good deal for you, Jack," the officer answered. "Don't blow it."

Finally, and with some difficulty, the woman and the police officer got Jack into the cafeteria and sat him at a table in a remote corner. It was the middle of the morning, so most of the breakfast crowd had already left, and the lunch bunch had not yet arrived. The manager strode across the cafeteria and stood by his table.

"What's going on here, Officer?" he asked. "What is all this. Is this man in trouble?"

"This lady brought this man in here to be fed," the policeman answered.

"Not in here!" the manager replied angrily. "Having a person like that here is bad for business."

Old Jack smiled a toothless grin. "See, lady. I told you so. Now if you'll let me go. I didn't want to come here in the first place."

The woman turned to the cafeteria manager and smiled. "Sir, are you familiar with Eddy and Associates, the banking firm down the street?"

"Of course, I am," the manager answered impatiently. "They hold their weekly meetings in one of my banquet rooms."

"And do you make a goodly amount of money providing food at these weekly meetings?"

"What business is that of yours?"

"I, sir, am Penelope Eddy, president and CEO of the company."

"Oh."

The woman smiled again.

"I thought that might make a difference." She glanced at the cop who was busy stifling a giggle.

"Would you like to join us in a cup of coffee and a meal, Officer?"

"No thanks, ma'am," the officer replied. "I'm on duty."

"Then, perhaps, a cup of coffee to go?" "Yes,

ma'am. That would be very nice." The cafeteria manager turned on his heel.

"I'll get your coffee for you right away, Officer."

The officer watched him walk away. "You certainly put him in his place," he said.

"That was not my intent. Believe it or not, I have a reason for all this."

She sat down at the table across from her amazed dinner guest. She stared at him intently. "Jack, do you remember me?"

Old Jack searched her face with his old, rheumy eyes. "I think so—I mean, you do look familiar."

"I'm a little older perhaps," she said. "Maybe I've even filled out more than in my younger days when you worked here, and I came through that very door, cold and hungry."

"Ma'am?" the officer said questioningly. He couldn't believe that such a magnificently turned out woman could ever have been hungry.

"I was just out of college," the woman began. "I had come to the city looking for a job, but I couldn't find anything. Finally, I was down to my last few cents and had been kicked out of my apartment. I walked the streets for days. It was February and I was cold and nearly starving. I saw this place and walked in on the off chance that I could get something to eat."

Jack lit up with a smile. "Now I remember," he said. "I was behind the serving counter. You came up and asked me if you could work for something to eat. I said that it was against company policy."

"I know," the woman continued. "Then you made me the biggest roast beef sandwich that I had ever seen, gave me a cup of coffee, and told me to go over to a corner table and enjoy it. I was afraid that you would get into trouble. Then, when I looked over, I saw you put the price of my food in the cash register I knew then that everthing would be all right."

"So you started your own business?" Old Jack said.

"I got a job that very afternoon. I worked my way up. Eventually I started my own business that, with the help of God, prospered." She opened her purse and pulled out a business card. "When you are finished here, I want you to pay a visit to a Mr. Lyons. He's the personnel director of my company. I'll go talk to him now and I'm certain he'll find something for you to do around the office." She smiled. "I think he might even find the funds to give you a little advance so that you can buy some clothes and get a place to live until you get on your feet. If you ever need anything, my door is always opened to you."

There were tears in the old man's eyes. "How can I ever thank you?" he said.

"Don't thank me," the woman answered. "To God goes the glory. Thank Jesus… He led me to you."

Outside the cafeteria, the officer and the woman paused at the entrance before going their separate ways.

"Thank you for all your help, Officer," she said.

"On the contrary, Ms. Eddy," he answered. "Thank you. I saw a miracle today, something that I will never forget. And. And thank you for the coffee."

As my wife sent this e-mail to friends, she concluded by saying,

> If you have missed knowing me, you have missed nothing. If you have missed some of my emails, you might have missed a laugh.
>
> But if you have missed knowing my *Lord and Savior, Jesus Christ*, you have missed everything in the world.

Have a wonderful day. May God bless you always! And don't forget that when you "cast your bread upon the waters," you never know how it will be returned to you.

God is so big He can cover the whole world with his love and so small he can curl up inside your heart.

As you go through life and no matter what age you are right now, understand the joy of giving. I hope that you will take the time to outline a plan to be a bigger giver in the future. Give some of your time. Give lots of your love. Give your smile! Give your knowledge and understanding! Know that life is short, and it goes by like a snap of your fingers. Knowing that you receive such joy in giving, I hope that you will get creative in how you can give. *It is what life is all about!*

Giving of yourself in a loving, caring way as you go through life will have a positive influence on everyone you touch in your life. I know that when they talk about your "Dash" one of the things you will want to hear is; he/she was such a giver. Giving of their time, giving of their love in a way that touched everyone who ever had the pleasure of meeting her/him. I would hope that is what they will say about your "dash"!

4

Challenges in Life!

Life is not meant to be easy, but the rewards can far outweigh the difficulties. As we go through life, we will be challenged. The key is to understand that when God provides challenges in our life, he is testing our attitude, our flexibility, and our faith. Looking back on my life, I was faced with many challenges that would have made many people give up. I have even had people tell me that "Good heaven... I think I would have committed suicide if I had to go through what you have in your life."

> Dear brothers and sisters, whenever trouble comes your way, let it be an opportunity for joy. For when your faith is tested, your endurance has a chance to grow. So let it grow, for when your endurance is fully developed, you will be strong in character and ready for anything. (James 1:2–4)

Reflecting on my own life, I was not unlike anyone else. I wanted to be successful; in fact, I remember thinking that I should have a plan that would enable me to retire at thirty-five...what a big dreamer! I am today a bigger dreamer than most people could ever imagine. Life has taught me that you need to be a dreamer to really find out what God's plan is for your life. Dreaming involves the "fun of life." But what most people find out by being a dreamer is that it can actually be fun. It involves setting goals and being accountable, being disciplined, being positive, being optimistic.

Having tenacity and, most importantly, having an undying faith. Develop a neversay-die attitude. What I found out is that when a door is closed in your life, God will open new doors. You need to look for them. God will lead you to his plan, but he also does not make it easy. I believe he really wants to test your faith as part of helping you find His plan for your life.

Do you put your faith in God or people? So as you set out to reach your goals and dreams, you will always be challenged along the way. I mean challenges happen like rain drops one after another. What do most people do in such circumstances? They quit! They give up on their dream. They settle for less, and their lives become mundane, boring, without excitement. They have given up on themselves and have lost their faith. They end up listening to people and stop having faith in God. When you give up, you will not find God's plan for your life.

I was one that just refused to give up. However, what I also came to realize was that no matter how hard I tried to succeed relying on my own efforts alone, it was never enough. It was when I learned to call on God for wisdom and knowledge, and turn my challenges over to him knowing that he was a big-enough God to handle anything. This is when I learned what God's plan was for my life. I learned that in asking the Lord to become my savior, he also became my partner. I was able to understand what plan he had for my life, but also, I came to understand what a joy the journey was even through all the challenges. The challenges became part of the joy of victory.

One of the companies that I started was Kings River Expeditions. Over a ten-year time frame, we developed the Kings River Expeditions into one of the best white-water rafting experiences in the US. At the end of each season, we usually took our staff down another river somewhere in California or Oregon. One of our favorite rivers is the Rogue River in Southern Oregon. There was a fifty-five-mile section that we would take five days to complete going about eleven miles each day. Seeing the wildlife and just getting totally away from roads, cars, and civilization was fantastic. It was a trip that always refreshed the soul.

WHAT'S LIFE ALL ABOUT?

What is funny is that we have made that trip thirteen times, but the one trip that we always come back to talk about the most was the trip that we made the first week in August of 1976. In August, the weather on the Rogue River is usually hot with the temperature in the upper nineties. No need to bring warm clothes or rain gear, right? Wrong! For this particular trip, this part of Oregon had a record rainfall for this whole week in August. It was cold, and we had no tents and certainly were not prepared for this type of weather. On our rafts we had large plastic tarps that we laid down in the front of the boat where we packed all our clothes and sleeping bags. The tarp then was folded back over the gear to keep it dry while we went through the rapids. These tarps were the only means that we had to get out of the rain for five days. We would stake out these tarps, so they were about three feet over the top of us, and we slept under them. So we called one the Rogue River Hilton, one the Rogue River Holiday Inn, and the smaller ones the Rogue River Motel 6. We made a big fire, we laughed, we just made the best with what we had, and we refused to let rain and cold ruin our trip.

The last day on the river it was extremely cold, and the wind and the rain were coming down hard. We were headed downriver, but it seemed that for every stroke of the paddle we made, the wind actually took us back upriver.

We thought that we would never get off that river. You know what is so funny? That was the only trip that it really rained on us in thirteen trips, but that is the trip that we have relived over and over talking about our experiences on the Rogue River. We have laughed and reminisced about that trip over and over. Remembering how we had to rig a dry place to sleep… Yes, the Rogue River Hilton and Holiday Inn. Those have become fun and fond memories of how we all worked together to make the best out of a miserable situation with the weather. So if life throws you a lemon, just decide to make lemonade and be thankful for the challenges. The challenges will build your character.

> "And without faith it is impossible to please God, because anyone who comes to him must believe that he exists and that he rewards those who earnestly seek him" (Heb. 11:6).

I learned that your attitude regarding your faith truly helps to determine your attitude in life when overcoming challenges. Because you know you are on the path to victory before you arrive. Faith is the key to overcoming your challenges in life. Turn them over to the Lord and know through faith that he is a loving, caring God and no challenge is too large for him.

When you turn your challenges over to God, it would be like playing a basketball game knowing that you were going to win the game, even if at half time, your team was down by twenty points. You see it would not matter what challenges you had to go through if you knew you had already won the game. Being down by twenty points would only be a temporary setback. You go back out in the second half with joy in your heart knowing you were going to win the game. You must do your part and work for it. You are not going to be able to just do nothing and win.

Far too many people in life do not believe they can win. They do not understand the power of faith. Many Christians still need to learn this lesson. They claim to be Christians, but they lose their faith and more often than not will simply give into their current circumstances. Perhaps they do not know how much the Lord loves them and that he will help them win their game if they will only refuse to give in to discouragement and hold on to faith.

> "For I say, through the grace given unto me, to every man that is among you, not to think [of himself] more highly than he ought to think; but to think soberly, according as God hath dealt to every man the measure of faith" (Rom. 12:3 KJV).

WHAT'S LIFE ALL ABOUT?

Learn to Enjoy the Journey, because the Destination May Become Secondary

When you have a dream, it is usually based on reaching a certain destination or reaching a certain level of success—the biggest mistake that most people make, and I must admit that I have been guilty of this. You need to realize that each and every day is a blessing. You need to enjoy each day to the fullest on your journey. So many times, we get caught up in where we are trying to end up that we forget how blessed we are each day and do not enjoy the journey. The journey should be the fun part, the challenging part, the part the makes you cry, laugh, and appreciate life.

I received this poem in an e-mail; it was written by a teenager with cancer who had only a short time to live. She wanted to see how many people would receive her poem. The email was sent out by a medical doctor who honored her last wish.

You will see in this poem that this teenager understood a great deal of what life is all about. Her poem is entitled "Slow Dance." I know you will enjoy and relate to this poem's meaning.

Slow Dance

> Have you ever watched kids
> On a merry-go-round?
> Or listened to the rain
> Slapping on the ground?
> Ever followed a butterfly's erratic flight?
> Or gazed at the sun into the fading night?
> You better slow down.
> Don't dance so fast. Time is short.
> The music won't last.
> Do you run through each day
> On the fly?
> When you ask How are you?
> Do you hear the reply?
> When the day is done
> Do you lie in your bed
> With the next hundred chores
> Running through your head? You'd better slow down

Don't dance so fast.
Time is short.
The music won't last
Ever told your child,
We'll do it tomorrow?
And in your haste,
Not see his sorrow?
Ever lost touch,
Let a good friendship die
'Cause you never had time
To call and say 'Hi'
You'd better slow down.
Don't dance so fast.
Time is short.
The music won't last.
When you run so fast to get somewhere
You miss half the fun of getting there.
When you worry and hurry through your day,
It is like an unopened gift…
Thrown away.
Life is not a race.
Do take it slower
Hear the music
Before the song is over.

This teenager understands that it is not the destination that is important it is the journey. Enjoy each day. Be thankful for the sun coming up. Be thankful that you have something to eat each day. Be thankful for all the little things that so many of us just take for granted. Love life, love people and do not be in such a hurry. Take the time to smell the roses each day.

While on your journey, have fun and count your blessings every day. You need to be thankful; you need to develop your love factor. For many, the journey is the real joy, not the destination.

As God closes one door, he opens another one. Learn to recognize doors that he opens for you.

I truly believe that as you face challenges that bring doubt and uncertainty in your life and your life plan, it is probably God closing a door on you. Get excited, since you were not supposed to go through that door. Be excited because another door will be there for you to go through that is the right door for your life plan.

Have Joy in Failure!

How have you analyzed your failures in life? Most people do not handle failure very well. Many blame others or circumstances, the economy, or even God. You do not have to blame anyone or anything; look at your failures as learning experiences. Give thanks to God for the lessons learned. Be thankful for your failures

"Failure is only an opportunity to begin again more intelligently" (Henry Ford).

If everything you ever attempted worked and you never had a failure… it would make you a very dull person. You would not be appreciative of hard work and the importance of persistence and the attitude of never giving up. You are probably thinking, *No, I would have liked to have never had a failure!* No, because failures give you perspective. Failures will give you gratitude. They give you character, understanding, passion, and they give you appreciation for the work and dedication that it takes to reach success. So always get excited about failing and get right back up again and charge. Just refuse to let a failure bring you down in your attitude about life. *Get excited!*

You need to learn to rely on Jesus Christ. You will find that this is the secret that will always take you through those hardships in life. Having faith in the Lord is the answer.

> "I have learned the secret of being happy at any time in everything that happens. I can do all things through Christ, because he gives me strength" (Phil. 4:13).

Never look at failure as being a negative in your life. Walt Disney filed bankruptcy three times in his life. But he never gave up. He always kept his dream alive and his positive attitude motivating him, and accepted his failures as positive learning experiences. So many of us give up once we have a failure and become complacent and are not willing to try again. The one thing that I believe in is that by developing a loving spirit for life, it becomes much easier to understand the joy of the trials and tribulations of life. Always be thankful and be as excited in the bad times as you are in the good times. If you will practice this attitude, you will learn what your "why" is for your life and *what life is all about.*

Always remember that relationships are the most important aspect of your life, not things

> Jesus said, "Life is not measured by how much one owns." (Luke 12:15)

> We brought nothing into this world, and we can take nothing out of it. (1 Tim. 6:7)

You need to learn to lean on the Lord and his stability rather than your own.

> "I know what I am planning for you," says the Lord.

> "I have good plans for you, not plans to hurt you. I will give you hope and a good future." (Jer. 29:11)

So we will not be afraid even if the earth shakes, or the mountains fall into the sea. (Ps. 46:2)

You need to understand that the pain that you suffered in the past with your failures needs to be left in the past, learn from those lessons, and get excited about moving forward in your future. Do not live in your past.

> Apostle Paul wisely wrote, "Forgetting those things which are behind, and reaching forth unto those things which are before, I press on" (Phil. 3:13–14).

Do you understand that the fear of failure is what causes most people to fail before they event start? You attract to you what you think about and if you are thinking and fearing about failing all the time, guess what? You will probably fail! Concentrate on where you are going and stop worrying about failing.

> "The fear of man is a dangerous trap" (Prov. 29:25).

The Lord will test your faith and you know what happens to most people? They give up too soon as they question their faith. Success was just

WHAT'S LIFE ALL ABOUT?

around the corner. The most important thing you need to remember is that with God on your team, you cannot lose, so why do you worry about it and why would you ever give up?

> "A lazy fellow has trouble all through life" (Prov. 15:19).

Why is it that we will continue to try it "our way" and ignore God's advice? The Bible provides us a detailed outline of how we should live our life. He provides instruction and guidance for how we should live our life regarding our work, our home, and our relationships. The Bible will give you a road map on how you should approach every situation in your life. Why do we ignore it?

> "There is a way that seems right to a man, but in the end it leads to death" (Prov. 14:12).

The major reason that we would ignore the teachings of the Bible is that we either have not been led to the Lord, or if we have been led to the Lord, it was not drilled into our thick skull that this is it, this is the answer. The Bible provides all the answers. We always tend to want to go back to the thinking that we can do it on our own. If you will come to truly understand the power of the Lord and that it is his plan for your life that counts, not your plan. If you get this, then you will start to understand how magnificent life is and that he wants your life to be filled with joy and happiness and riches. When we fail to understand that we need God's road map, the Bible, and insist on trying it our way is asking for trouble.

Do you think that maybe your failures were brought about because you were trying to do it your way?

> Proverbs 28:13 says, "Anyone who refuses to admit his mistakes can never be successful. But if he confesses and forsakes them, he gets another chance."

I believe that if we understand what life is all about, that we will first understand that God has a plan for our life, he has given us a road map in how to find our true path in life as given to us in his teachings from the Bible. If we accept this as a fact, then why would we not want to follow that path?

> Proverbs 20:30 tells us, "Sometimes it takes a

painful situation to make us change our ways."

When will you admit that you do not have the answers? You need to ask the Lord for your plan.

Learn to be flexible… Always get back up when you get knocked down!

> "Consider it all joy, my brethren, when you encounter various trails; Knowing that the testing of your faith produces endurance. And let endurance have its perfect result, that you may be perfect and complete, lacking in nothing" (James 1:2–4).

This scripture reminds me of a true story in my life. At one time in my past, I became an Amway distributor. It was actually a great experience, and I met many wonderful people working to become free of a mundane job. My wife and I attended a conference one year and one of the guest speakers was a very successful distributor. We listened to him tell the story of how he was in California speaking at a conference several years ago and decided to buy a brand-new Cadillac and drive it back to North Carolina where he lived. He was planning to stop along the way to visit individuals that were in is Amway business. As he tells the story, he was driving through the Mojave Desert about 2:00 a.m. in his brand-new Cadillac. Suddenly, the car just stopped. It would not start again. It was not out of gas and he had no idea what was wrong. Now what would you do in this situation? Besides kicking the car and taking the Lords name in vain, that is. Brand-new Cadillac, 2:00 a.m. in the morning, and no one traveling in the middle of the Mojave Desert! No cell phones back then and no emergency call boxes. What did he do? He got out of the car and looked up into the sky and said, *"Thank You Lord for something fantastic is about to happen."* One trucker went flying by, did not stop. Much later, a car came by, but it did not stop either. After about two hours, at 4:00 a.m., a trucker stopped and picked him up and took him to the nearest town. He was able to stay at a motel and get a tow truck to go back and get his car the next morning. He was very grateful to the trucker and on the drive to town they were able to have a very positive conversation. He was able to talk to this trucker about life and opportunities. Yes, this trucker became a distributor that grew and grew in the Amway business to the point where the truckers Amway business was ultimately responsible for providing over $250,000 of annual income to the stranded owner of the Cadillac. God had a plan for these two to meet and have a lifelong relationship that was positive for each of them.

WHAT'S LIFE ALL ABOUT?

I have never forgotten this true story. When things seem on the surface to be a disaster, I look to the sky and say, *"Thank you, Lord for something fantastic is about to happen!"* If you develop a strong covenant with God, he will lead you where you need to be. You might not understand it at the time, but as time goes on, you will find yourself saying okay, now I understand why you had me go through that experience. You wanted me to learn that lesson. Now it all makes since. You can see the big picture that God has for your life. Many times, we have a hard time seeing or understanding it at the time. We had to experience certain trials and tribulations. The most important thing to remember is to be thankful, have a loving spirit, and have a positive attitude about all things that happen in your life. Especially the times that you feel are negative experiences. Everything happens for a reason. I believe that God has a divine plan for my life and for your life. As certain doors are closed in your life, he will open much larger doors to go through that will lead you to your ultimate destination. Too many people do not recognize the doors that are being opened and, therefore, never journey to explore the opportunities that the Lord is providing. If you believe that God does have a plan for your life, wouldn't it make sense to start looking for the doors he will open for you? Move forward with faith that his plan will bring you the most joy and happiness in your life. And remember that you will get to serve others all along the way.

> "And we know that God causes everything to work together for the good of those who love God and are called according to his purpose for them" (Rom. 8:28).

God Is Always There Ready to Help

This reminds me of something that happened to a good friend of mine, the director of the Fresno Rescue Mission. He related to me this something that God did for him, and then I realized that you can always count on God.

The director of the rescue mission received a phone call from another nonprofit in Fresno that was serving battered women. They asked if, by any chance, the rescue mission had any extra meat they could spare as their facility had not had any meat to serve in over sixty days. The director of the rescue mission said, "Yes, I will have our staff pull some meat out of our freezer for you to pick up." When the staff person was pulling out the meat for this purpose, he noticed that the freezer was all frozen up and needed repair. So all the rescue mission's meat was pulled from the freezer. Well, you know what happened? Yes, the other agency took all the meat that the rescue mission had. The director of the rescue mission received a call from the mission's head chef who told him, "We have no meat." He had the chef call the maintenance staff and he was told what had happened. The chef then asked the director, "Should I call them and go get some of our meat back?" The director said, "No, let's pray on it." One hour after praying on their need for meat, the director of the rescue mission received a call from Stockton Naval Shipyard. The caller proceeded to say, "Can your rescue mission use any meat?" He said that we have seventy thousand pounds of meat that will not fit on our ship headed to Iraqi. The response was "Yes, we can use it." The director of the rescue mission was able to secure two large refrigerated trucks to pick all seventy thousand pounds of meat up. Now the Fresno Rescue Mission had no room to store seventy thousand pounds of meat. So he had meat delivered to the rescue mission in Turlock, Merced, and once it arrived in Fresno, was able to fill up over nine nonprofit organizations' freezers with meat. He not only filled both rescue missions' freezers but had to rent two more large freezer spaces to store the remaining meat. After this was over, the director of the Fresno Rescue Mission happened to call the navy shipyard and ask him how you happened to call us to see if we needed meat. He replied, "We have about twenty-five phone books here and just happened to pick up Fresno and saw you had a rescue mission, so I called you first." Wow, and if that was not God at work, I do not know what else to believe. God answers prayers, and in this case, he answered a prayer immediately. Truly God at work.

Develop a Proper Perspective

I received the following story in an e-mail one day and am not sure who to give credit to. But it provides a great lesson to be learned about having the proper perspective in life.

Like a Garbage Truck

"How often do you let other people change your mood? Do you let a bad driver, rude waiter, curt boss, or an insensitive employee ruin your day?
Five years ago, I learned this lesson in the back of a taxicab in Indianapolis. Here's what happened:
I hopped in a taxi, and we took off for the

airport. We were driving in the right lane when suddenly a black car jumped out of a parking space right in front of us. My taxi driver slammed on his brakes, skidded, and missed the other car by just inches! The driver of the other car whipped his head around and started yelling at us. My taxi driver just smiled and waved at the guy.

So I asked, "Why did you just do that? This guy almost ruined your car and sent us to the hospital!"

This is when my taxi driver taught me what I now call, "The Law of the Garbage Truck." He explained that many people are like garbage trucks. They run around full of garbage, full of frustration, full of anger, and full of disappointment. As their garbage piles up, they need a place to dump it and sometimes they'll dump it on you. Don't take it personally. Just smile, wave, wish them well, and move on. Don't take their garbage and spread it to other people at work, at home, or on the streets.

The bottom line is that successful people do not let garbage trucks take over their day. Life's too short to wake up in the morning with regrets, so…

Love the people who treat you right. Pray for the ones who don't.

Keep a sweet, sweet spirit in your heart and above all keep the faith."

I also received the following story one day in an e-mail. It did not have the name of the author attached, but I thought what it a great lesson as to what life is all about:

> One day, the father of a very wealthy family took his son on a trip to the country with the express purpose of showing him how poor people live.
>
> They spent a couple of days and nights on the farm of what would be considered a very poor family.
>
> On their return from their trip, the father asked his son, "How was the trip?"

"It was great, Dad."

"Did you see how poor people live?" the father asked.

"Oh yeah," said the son.

"So tell me, what did you learn from the trip?" asked the father.

The son answered: "I saw that we have one dog and they had four. We have a pool that reaches to the middle of our garden and they have a creek that has no end. We have imported lanterns in our garden and they have the stars at night. Our patio reaches to the front yard and they have the whole horizon. We have a small piece of land to live on and they have fields that go beyond our sight. We have servants who serve us, but they serve others. We buy our food, but they grow theirs. We have walls around our property to protect us. they have friends to protect them."

The boy's father was speechless.

Then his son added, "Thanks, Dad, for showing me how poor we are."

Isn't perspective a wonderful thing? Makes you wonder what would happen if we all gave thanks for everything we have, instead of worrying about what we don't have. Appreciate everything you have, especially your friends! "Life is too short and friends are too few."

5

What Is Your "Why"?

Have you given deep thought as to why you were born and what your purpose is here on earth? Most people are not sure. Even most Christians who already believe in God are not sure what their "why" is in life. One of the things that I hope to accomplish in this book is to provide you with a road map to explore how you might start identifying your "why" and guide you to greater contentment, happiness and joy.

Most people have a hard time understanding that they have a "why," even though they might be a Christian, go to church, and do their best to live "a Christian life." They do not truly understand what that means. Even if they have an idea what it means, they may find it difficult to determine what their "why is, or even understand what it means to find their God-given purpose.

The preceding paragraph begs the question, if God has a plan for everyone's life, and that plan was established before they were ever born, why is it that most people get sidetracked and never discover the "why" that God planned for them? In my opinion, as Christians, we do a very poor job of teaching what it means to be a Christian. If you accept Christ as your savior, then doesn't it make sense to accept Christ as your partner in life and listen to what he teaches us from the word of God in the Bible? If you ask for God to reveal to you his plan for you and you start to be aware of opportunities, and you move forward with faith, it will happen.

The key is that you need to move forward with faith. Have an understanding that God will lead you to his plan for you. At times, your faith will be tested, and you may tend to listen to the wrong people. Always remember that God gives you free will. When making decisions, ask yourself, what would Jesus do?

I have always been an entrepreneur, having started over ten businesses. Right out of college, I wanted to own my own business and started my first travel agency. Talk about challenges, finding enough capital, finding the right personnel, developing a new business, developing a budget, a business plan, and a marketing plan. You talk about wondering what your "why" is… starting that first business was exciting, but also was very scary at the same time. Was this God's plan for my life? This was not God's end plan for my life, but it was his plan for me to experience the ups and downs of starting these businesses and being successful in some and failing in others. It was his plan to give me the firsthand knowledge of lessons I would need to know that would ultimately lead me to his master plan.

I realized that I loved the challenge of the "new", of starting something from nothing and seeing what you could create. I found that I was an entrepreneur, and once you have the entrepreneur mindset it is very hard to accept a "job". Not that there is anything wrong with a job, but I found that having an entrepreneur mindset and then having a job was very hard. I have had a few jobs in my earlier years, and I was an excellent employee. I was never late, and I always gave a 110 percent effort in anything that I did. Being an entrepreneur, I became a big dreamer and wanted more than what I thought a job would provide for me and my family. Having started over ten companies, I learned that God truly did have a plan for my life, and each of my failures and successes were learning lessons for what he had planned for my life. As I was going through life working to find the right business to become successful, I was just like a lot of people. Working hard, thinking that if I can just get this business off the ground I will have arrived. I really did not know for sure what God had in mind for me, because I really was not looking or thinking about God's plan. I was looking to establish my own plan. It was centered on what I could do. My efforts, me…me…me! At this time in my life, I did not really understand that God had a plan for my life, and no matter how much I thought it was about me, it was not.

I was a Christian and had accepted Jesus Christ as my savior years earlier like many *born again Christians*, but I really did not get it. I thought, "Great, I believe in God, and I am going to heaven," but was totally clueless about what it really meant to believe in God. I mean, truly believe, with a knowing faith

WHAT'S LIFE ALL ABOUT?

that God created me for a purpose and that he had a plan for my life before I was even born. Once I realized what it meant to become a true Christian and have total faith in God and not to depend on my own knowledge or efforts is when I really got excited about life and looked forward to each day and what that day would bring toward developing my life that was based on his plan for me.

> "Everything has already been decided. It was known long ago what each person would be. So, there's no use arguing with God about your destiny" (Eccles. 6:10).

Aren't you tired of doing it all on your own? Think about this for one minute. If you believe in God, and that God created Earth and the heavens, then don't you think that his plan for your life is probably the best plan for you? For your happiness, for your true joy of life, and for just being alive? When you think of all the dreamers and the visionaries and the inventors of the world, where do you think those dreams and visions came from? Do you think maybe God had something to do with it? People tell me all the time, "Boy, you sure lucked out!" No, after so many failures and trials and tribulations, I became a believer that the dreams and visions that I had in my life were given to me by God, and I needed to have faith in God that he would see me through the challenges. I finally got it; it was not me. It was not my dream, my vision; those were all gifts from God. God was providing them to help me along the right road to become the person and fulfill the plan that God had in mind for me before I was even born. If you get this, you will not be able to sleep because of the excitement of knowing you now know that you know that you know.

> "ARISE [from the depression and prostration in which circumstances have kept you—rise to a new life]! Shine (be radiant with the glory of the Lord), for your light has come, and the glory of the Lord has risen upon you!" (Isa. 60:10).

Being an entrepreneur, I was always looking for opportunities where I could have my own business. I had no idea where the Lord would take me. In fact, ten years before Full Circle Energy Inc. and the Remarkable Technologies Inc. if someone would have told me that I would end up cofounding Full Circle Energy and being the founder of Remarkable Technologies Inc.

I would not have believed it. That God would have me leading so many inventors and engineers in developing cutting-edge technologies! No way! That Full Circle Energy Inc. would become the leader in the world in taking garbage to clean renewable energy—again, would not have believed it. That Remarkable Technologies would develop the most efficient technologies in water desalination, sewage treatment, transportation, food production, energy production, and so many more. I would have asked them, what have they been smoking?

Just when I thought that God had truly led me to his plan for my life, I started on another journey of trials and tribulations. Let me explain.

I am currently the cofounder and CEO of Full Circle Energy Inc, the leader in waste-to-energy technology. My introduction into the waste-to-energy industry was only by the grace of God. Some would say simply by accident. But I believe everything happens for a reason, and most of those reasons are leading you to your destiny and the plan that God has for your life. My partner and I spent over fifteen years looking for the proper funding to take Full Circle Energy Inc. to its current position of number one, yet we experienced one set back after another. For instance, the Lord led my partner and I to the right people according to his plan…but some of those people were for "training purposes only" in God's plan for my life.

The pain and the challenges we faced along the way were unbelievable. I know that most people would have given up after the first five years. During fifteen years of focusing and believing in a dream to bring to the world technologies that would change the world for the better, the Lord tested our faith almost every day. From day to day, not knowing if we were going to be able to raise enough money to keep going was just one of the challenges we faced. Fifteen years is a long time to keep faith in a dream that many times looked like we should just throw in the towel. We never lost faith and never considered giving up. Knowing that the Lord had a plan and that he would test our worthiness and faithfulness repeatedly made the journey so worthwhile!

During this venture, the Lord prepared us in knowledge and wisdom; we were introduced to the right people. When I look back and see how Full Circle Energy came together, it could have only happened because of divine intervention. I truly believe that because we had miracle after miracle kept us in business for over fifteen years.

> "Therefore the Lord will wait, that He may be
> gracious to you; and therefore He will be exalted,

WHAT'S LIFE ALL ABOUT?

that He may have mercy on you… Blessed are all
those who wait for Him" (Isa. 30:18).

Most companies do not last three years, and a larger number do not make it to five years. Fifteen years working to keep everything together, it only happened because the Lord had a plan. If we needed to be introduced to a world-class scientist or engineer in our field, it happened. Time and time again, the Lord delivered the right people to us that we needed from the technical side of our business or the right people to bring in the financing that we needed to move forward.

> "If any of you lacks wisdom, he should ask God,
> who gives generously to all without finding fault,
> and it will be given to him" (James 1:5 NIV).

I was fifty-two years old when I finally realized my "why" in life. I was to be a part of establishing Full Circle Energy Inc. as the world leader in changing the world for the better by bringing a cutting-edge technology to clean up landfills and generate clean renewable energy from the many waste streams that we have been producing for years and years that have been contaminating our water and polluting our land and air.

I developed a passion for it. I had such a thirst for knowledge in this industry that I spent endless hours researching everything I could about waste-to-energy using thermal technologies. I asked the Lord for knowledge and wisdom to pursue this passion for playing a role in changing the world by providing a technology that would clean up waste streams like landfills (garbage), spent tires, sewage sludge, agricultural waste, hospital waste, and toxic waste streams.

Today, looking back, it is so easy to see what God had in mind for me and how I could play a role in helping his planet and people. I understood as things went wrong, it was only the Lord closing a door that he knew we should not go through and then he would open a door that he knew we needed to go through.

But hold on. The funding that we thought we had ended up not happening. So after fifteen years of working hard, developing the business plan to change the world to rid the world of garbage, again God closed a door. This was a door that we just knew was right, and they provided proof of funds of ten billion dollars. Yes, ten billion. We executed a contract and the investor was going to bring all the funding we needed to launch Full Circle Energy.

God knew that this investor was not the right person for us to be in business with, and the funding fell through. So what did I do, as many would have wanted to commit suicide? I looked to God and said, "Thank you, God, something fantastic is about to happen."

Moving beyond your understanding! After fifteen years of struggles working to secure our funding, and then believing you found it, to have it not be there, for most people would have been the last straw.

What I have learned through all of this is God will absolutely direct you to "His plan" for your life, not your plan. So in asking, "Okay, God, what do you have in mind now?"

Shortly after we realized that this funding was not going to happen, I was introduced to an inventor. This inventor had been very successful in the past with a couple of his inventions but had been taken advantage of from venture capitalists. He calls them vulture capitalists. To be honest with you, they are vulture capitalists. They will try to secure or steal the majority of an inventor's technology because of greed and power. This inventor was actually working on over forty various technologies. Every one of these technologies had the potential to dominate markets, and each had market potential in the billions of dollars. The most exciting aspect of all these technologies is that they were all technologies that would help mankind. They would drastically reduce cost to the end consumer and, at the same time, provide great profits to the company.

So what God did in giving me his vision for his plan for my life was to start a new company, which I called Remarkable Technology Inc. So many of the technologies we were seeing were truly "remarkable." Was God's plan for me to oversee a company that had a fantastic waste-to-energy technology? That was only a very small part of the plan that he had in mind. What happened over the next five years? God has introduced me to many more inventors that all have technologies, in water desalination, wastewater treatment (sewage treatment), and in energy production. These included the most incredible solar technology that pays for itself in less than three years. In food production, in transportation, in financial services, in so many technologies. When you put them all together, they are so remarkable that we will truly change the world for the better. As all these inventors and technologists were being introduced to me, I was able to explain to them that our companies, Full Circle Energy Inc. and Remarkable Technologies Inc., were really God's businesses. I have dedicated all my talents to simply wanting to be a good steward of what he has developed. After sitting down and meeting so many of these inventors and sharing my story of how God has worked in developing his plan, they all wanted to be a part of it. They have all shared with me that they are not going to go anywhere else for funding. They believe in the concept of creating a business model that God would smile down on and bless. To always create a win-win-win scenario in business. As we were collecting many technologies we were also being introduced to many key management people whose collective talents would develop our two companies into what we believe will be the example that God wants all to see and all businesses to emulate.

How Do You Find Your "Why" and God's Plan for Your Life?

Let's take a moment to talk about you and your "why"! Do you know the real reason you are here? Do you have a passion for life and what you are doing in it? If not, it is my opinion that you have either not gone through doors that were opened to you or you did not recognize the opportunity, or were influenced by others.

If you feel that you are lost and have no clue of your "why," then you need to pray to God and ask him. You need to let him know that you want to know your "why" and you are willing to follow his teachings and to start dreaming again so God can reveal his plan. You also need to move forward from this day with an expectation with faith that if you ask God to set you on his plan for your life, you will not worry or be afraid to make changes in your life. Start working on you in becoming more Christ-like. Work on you by developing the love factor in your life, becoming the person that has the loving, caring, and joyous heart and is willing to become a giver. In other words, you need to get to "*God's basics.*"

I have to admit, I did not always think that God had a plan for my life or other people's life. I thought that because I would observe people wasting their life away with no plan, no ambition, and not having a caring attitude and then I realized that God gives us choices. We choose who we associate with, who we are influenced by. We choose our attitude! We decide to have enthusiasm or not to have enthusiasm about life. We choose our friends and who we associate with. One of the most important things that I hope to impart to you in this book is that you have control over your choices, and if you have not discovered your "why" yet, it might be because you have been influenced by the wrong people and have taken advice from the wrong people and thus made the wrong choices. What will help you get back on track and find your "why" is learning to trust in the Lord. If you have the feeling that you need to make changes in your life, it just might be the Lord opening a door you need to go through. If you believe that the Lord has a plan for your life, then you need to have faith that he will lead you to it. And once he leads you to it, he will lead you through it. In my case, it was fifteen years of learning, working hard, and never giving up. And when I once thought I was done, we went another five years. My dream was big, but it did not compare to God's dream and plans for my life. My wife reminded me repeatedly by telling me, "If the Lord led you to it, he will lead you through it."

> "I will instruct you and teach you in the way which you shall go; I will guide you with mine eyes" (Ps. 32:8).

In making the right choices in life, you need to understand that the Lord will help direct you. Your reading this book might be the one thing you needed for you to finally realize that you need to trust in the Lord to get back on track with his plan for your life. If you have been frustrated, worried, depressed about where you are in life, it is never too late to get back on track.

You also need to understand that when God opens a door for you to go through, it might lead to a failure. But it will not be a failure in God's eyes, as he sometimes leads you into situations that he wants you to learn from, and then he opens a door that will lead you back to his plan for you.

That is what happened to me. The Lord led me to so many experiences and failures but I always knew that everything happens for a reason. So get excited no matter what happens. If you move with faith and a firm trust in the Lord, you will be on track.

Start to dream again. Do not be afraid to make mistakes; cherish the learning experience. As you dream, the Lord will give you the right thoughts to lead you in the right direction. He will give you a vision, and then it is up to you to act on your dreams and vision. Always remember he will lead you to it and lead you through it. If you have been frustrated with your life, then I hope that you will read the information that I have shared in this book and just get excited about life. Life is so wonderful, and it was meant to be wonderful for you as well. Be ready for change, and I suggest that you evaluate your failures in the past and recognize the learning lessons there and get excited about those failures and then ask God through prayer to put you back on track.

I found this quote on choices, but do not know who to give credit to for

WHAT'S LIFE ALL ABOUT?

it. But it is true.

Choices: "Watch your thoughts; they become words. Watch your words; they become actions. Watch your actions; they become habits. Watch your habits; they become character. Watch your character; it becomes your destiny."

Every day, we are given the opportunity to wake up with a positive attitude and give thanks to the Lord for the day. Or we can get up with a negative attitude, be discouraged, and give off negative vibrations to those you meet. You have the right to make a positive decision in all that you do or make a negative decision in all that you do. I personally believe that if you want pure love and joy from life, you need to give life pure love and joy. Give love and joy to everything you do. Everything you think about, and especially give love and joy to all you meet. Yes, develop the love factor in your life. Make the decision to work on you. So many people think that they are okay that everyone else needs to make changes.

Right now, where are you in your life? If you do not know beyond a shadow of a doubt what your "why" is in life, then you need to understand that God has a plan for your life. It does not matter if you are twenty years old or eighty years old. If you have not accepted Christ to come into your life, that needs to be the first step. You need to ask God to open the doors that will lead you to your "why." You need to move forward on your personal life journey with faith and develop a personal relationship with God. Talk to him in prayer. Ask for wisdom and knowledge. Ask him to direct your life toward your "why." Just decide in accepting Christ that from here on out, he will become your best friend, your business partner, and your partner in life. I must tell you, he is like no partner you have ever had. If you ask God for help, you need to be ready for his direction and have faith that a new path for your life is probably coming from God. So do not be afraid. Go forward with your gut feelings and do not totally rely on advice from others, especially if they themselves do not know their own "why" in life. They might mean well, but God is the only one that truly knows what path you need to take. Once you understand how God works, you will get very excited looking for the clues or the advice, or the vision, or the dreams you have… coming from him! Consider some of the feelings or intuition you get sometimes, or just the gut feelings you have, where do you think they come from? Yes, from God! Have faith and go with your gut. I really think that gut feelings are another way of saying God's directions.

> "And the Lord shall guide you continually,
> and satisfy your soul in drought, and make fat your

bones; and you shall be like a watered garden, and like a spring of water, whose waters fail not" (Isa. 58:11).

Keys to Happiness and Finding Your "Why"

Have you ever stopped to think just how great life is? I think of the beauty of a mountain stream, or being on a warm ocean beach, or hiking on a mountain trail, or seeing the redwoods. Have you ever been to Yosemite? Seeing God's work in nature is so life invigorating you just feel like jumping with joy when you realize how wonderful life is.

What a joy just to be alive. If you have that attitude, but not yet sure what God's plan is for you…just having that grateful attitude for being alive is a great start.

Become a dreamer for that is the key to your "why"

"To accomplish great things we must not only act, but also dream, not only plan, but also believe."

"Every great achievement was a dream before someone of vision turned it into a reality" (Henry Kissinger).

If you are looking for God's plan for you, I believe that it starts with a dream. Never stop dreaming. I know that in my life I have been a big dreamer and always wanted to become successful, yet for most of my life, I did not really know what plan God had for me. You know what I found out was that God's plan for me was much larger than my biggest dream. Did God just send me a message one day and say, "Fred, okay, you have been a dreamer, so I am going to answer what you have always been looking for and grant you a bigger dream than you can imagine"? No, God's plan was indeed big, but for me to understand his plan, he had to test my faith and patience to help me develop a *stick-to-it* attitude. He put every roadblock you could ever imagine in my path testing my faith.

Another thing that I have learned that turning your problems over to the Lord and knowing without any doubt that he will provide the answer is another key. Never give up… The Lord will never let you down. Does he answer prayers instantly? Sometimes, but most of the time, he will test your faith. You will learn that it is in His timing not yours.

One time, we had a guest pastor at our church, and he explained that we are a microwave society and we want it NOW, but our God is a *Crockpot*

WHAT'S LIFE ALL ABOUT?

God, and he stews things over to make sure it is right

> Are you disappointed, discouraged and discontented with your present level of success? Are you secretly dissatisfied with your present status? Do you want to become a better and more beautiful person than you are today? Would you like to be able to really learn how to be proud of yourself and still not lose genuine humility? Then start dreaming! It is possible! You can become the person you have always wanted to be! (Robert H. Schuller)

I believe that this is true, since dreaming opens the door for the plan that God has for your life. Keep in mind that God's plan for your life may not mean that you will become rich with untold wealth. It just might mean he wants you to be rich with love and a caring attitude for others.

I have known individuals that had very little when it came to "things". They did not have a large home or a new car or did not have the funds to travel or have a large wardrobe, but they were so rich in love and kindness and caring for others that I believe they had more riches than the wealthiest man in town. I tell you this because so many people believe that one's dreams means money and wealth, and that is not always so. It can be, but if that is your dream, what are you going to do with your wealth? How will you affect people's lives in a positive way with your wealth, because let's face it, if you have a nice home, nice transportation, and a few toys, and are able to travel, what else is there? There are people and your relationships with those people. How do you treat people? How do you love people?

How have you developed the love factor in your life? Those are the true measure of riches. Use money to work to help people; do not use people to make money. Learn God's basics and apply them in all aspects of your life.

I realized that all money really belongs to the Lord anyway. We use it, we work for it, we dream about it, but if your dream is to make money to give, to give back to help people, that is the true joy of life and the Lord will use that to lead you to your "why." Why are you here? Once you realize your "*why*," a joy will come over you like no other you've ever experienced. Your will be able to affect everyone you meet in a positive way. So if your dream becomes all self-serving, you will probably become caught up in disbelief or discouragement and give up on reaching or understanding your "why" in life.

"Champions aren't made in the gyms. Champions are made from

something they have deep inside them—a desire, a dream, a vision" (Muhammad Ali).

You know people that have basically given up on life. They live day-to-day in a self-made rut. They might even tell you that "Yes, I was a dreamer once, wanted to change the world, but everything I did just got shot down, what is the use? Just going to put my time in here and retire."

I know that the Lord had a plan for their life, but what happened is that their dream was probably all self-motivated—"what I will have, what I can buy, what I can do for me." The Lord wants you to dream for what and how you can make a difference, how you can affect people's lives in a positive, loving way. If that is your motivation, he takes care of you along the way like you cannot believe. He has a joy of giving in his heart and he wants you to learn that is one of the keys in what life is all about. If you understand that, you will know that when you focus your efforts on helping others, the Lord loves to be a giver. He will bless you beyond your imagination. But if you are all about you, your dream probably got discouraged to the point where you just threw in the towel.

Is that you? Have you given up on your dream? What was your dream? What was the foundation of your dream? Was it based on your achievement, or was it based on reaching goals that would have a major impact on helping others and making a difference? If your dream is on you succeeding that is okay but turn that success into being able to help others in some way.

The good news is that it is never too late. I discovered the power of dreaming again at fifty, and it turned my attitude into a childlike joy and I became so excited about life. The Lord led me to become a leader of two companies that truly will change the world and affect people's life's all over the world. In this process, I recognized that whatever I did, I would ask the Lord for wisdom and knowledge to become the leader that I needed to become with the vision to direct these companies to accomplish things that would make a huge difference in changing the world to help mankind.

Every time that I would get sidetracked and start thinking about me and my family, he would direct me back to what the plan he had for my life. I knew that my thoughts and actions and my focus were on how to solve problems to help people. With your focus on others, the Lord will also take very good care of you and your family as well. I understood that the companies I would lead would be in position to not only help people with environmental problems; provide clean potable water; provide the best wastewater treatment solutions for the world; provide food production, transportation, and so much more.

WHAT'S LIFE ALL ABOUT?

These companies would also earn tremendous profits while drastically reducing cost to the end consumer. I started to get excited about what our companies could do to use some of those profits to help people.

We decided that a percentage of the profits needed to go to the foundation that we created. We called our foundation The Extended Hands of Christ Foundation.

Was this plan an easy road? No...no...no, I have to tell you, we spent fifteen long years working hard to raise money to keep the company from going under. Every time, over a fifteen-year time frame when it looked like we had done all we could to keep everything going, I called upon the Lord. He led us to the right person or persons to provide additional funding to keep the company going. There were so many times that we needed money on a day to pay the phone bill or it would be shut off, or to pay another critical bill. What did I do? I prayed and called upon the Lord to bring us the funds we needed, and every time after praying, I would get a call from one of our investors that would ask me, "Is there any chance that my brother could make an investment?" "Yes, there is!" The Lord would answer our prayers every time. This went on for over fifteen years. God had a plan for my life. He is a God that cares. He is a forgiving God. He is a God that hears your prayers, and he answers prayers. God always brought to us the right people for the companies, and God not only brought us the right people, but the very best people for what the companies needed at that time. God is now in charge of our HR department.

Full Circle Energy and Remarkable Technologies have experienced so many miracles over a combined fifteen-year period most people cannot believe it. Sometimes it is even hard for us to believe it, but there is no other possible answer but to know that our two companies have been divinely guided. Every time that we faced a critical period or situation that would have prevented us from being able to continue, we called upon the Lord for help and he provided the need.

Does God Have a Plan for Your Life?

"Without faith, hope and trust, there is no promise for the future, and without a promising future, life has no direction, no meaning and no justification."

> "'For I know the plans I have for you,' says the Lord. 'They are plans for good and not for evil, to give you a future and a hope...You will find me

when you seek me, if you look for me in earnest'" (Jer. 29:11, 13 LB).

When you truly look to the Lord for help in identifying what your "why" is and what his plan is for your life, I want to remind you that you will find the doors will start to open! But you need to be on the lookout for those doors and have faith to open the door and go through it. This might mean a career change like it was for me. It might mean just start developing the love factor in your life and then opportunities will come your way. Start to work on God's basics in you and then you will need to go forward with faith and determination and have a happy loving heart. Give thanks to the Lord; ask for his help in wisdom and knowledge. By keeping the faith, you will not believe what he will bring into your life.

True possibility…

> "Jesus looked at them intently and said, 'Humanly speaking, it is impossible. But with God everything is possible'" (Matt. 19:26).

6

Developing Your Character for God's Plan

Some More of God's Basics!

Integrity

As you start your journey to find and develop your "why," it will be important for you to evaluate and develop your character. Are you a person that has integrity? Some people try to portray a public image of trustworthiness and integrity, but it is what comes from the heart and the inside which reveals your true integrity.

Dictionary's definition of integrity: "Uprightness of character; honesty, unimpaired state; soundness; undivided or unbroken state; completeness."

Have the courage to say no. Have the courage to face the truth. Do the right thing because it is right. These are some of the magic keys to living your life with integrity.

> "Better a poor man who lives with integrity than a rich man who distorts right and wrong" (Prov. 28:6).

After I graduated from college and started my first travel agency in Santa Maria, California, it seems I would always cross paths with successful businessmen that did not have integrity. I always wondered how they became successful. As time went by, I learned that they were not really happy. They did not a have great relationship with their family. Most did not have any relationship with God, and though on the surface looked successful they were miserable in real life. They really did not care about people. Most of them took advantage of their employees and did not have any of the elements of the love factor working in their life. In the ten businesses that I started and the many, many contacts in business that I have met, I found many of these lost souls in business, who placed so much value on the almighty dollar. They did not understand the value of the love factor in their lives or in how they treated their employees, their customers or their relationships with people in general or even their family.

> "He who walks with integrity walks securely" (Prov. 10:9).

Sometimes, it would cause me to ask God. "How did these people ever become successful?" I found that even though many were successful financially they were not successful in life. For what is money all about if it is not to help people, to make a difference in other peoples' lives? Many of these businessmen were so entranced with *making money* they did not have a clue what life is really all about.

> "The Lord shall judge the people; judge me, O Lord, according to my righteousness, and according to mine integrity that is in me" (Ps. 7:8).

You might know people like this; you might have been like this, or maybe you still are. When you start to wonder what life is all about and what is your real "why" in life. Is it really to make all the money you can, no matter what it does to others—your employees, business associates, customers, or family?

> "Let integrity and uprightness preserve me; for I wait on thee" (Ps. 25:21).

Life is made up of little choices. As you make your choices in life regarding your work, your business, your friends, your business associates, or your family, are you willing to make those decisions with integrity? I have found that if you make every decision with integrity and with a love factor in your heart God will be pleased and you will be on the path to finding your "why."

WHAT'S LIFE ALL ABOUT?

"The Lord demands fairness in every business deal. He established this principle" (Prov. 16:11).

Enthusiasm

Enthusiasm is one of those intangible things about developing your character that is very important and really is part of the love factor. Enthusiasm is contagious just being around someone who has enthusiasm will bring a smile.

"Life's blows cannot break a person whose spirit is warmed at the fire of enthusiasm" (Norman Vincent Peale).

Enthusiasm is a feeling and an attitude, but it's also a skill. And like any other skill, if it is continually practiced and exercised, it gets better. If it does not get exercised, then it will degrade. Enthusiasm rarely comes naturally, and it must be the result of conscious effort. Practicing the ability to use enthusiasm can keep you excited and driven even in horrible circumstances.

Enthusiasm and energy are very closely linked. Being energetic makes it far more likely for you to be enthusiastic and enthusiasm can literally create the energy you need to get going. This may sound like a catch-22, but it isn't.

> Enthusiasm is the yeast that makes your hopes shine to the stars. Enthusiasm is the sparkle in your eyes, the swing in your gait. The grip of your hand, the irresistible surge of will and energy to execute your ideas. (Henry Ford)

> Success consists of going from failure to failure without loss of enthusiasm. (Winston Churchill)

As you are searching for your "why" and God opens doors, it is very important that you go through that door with enthusiasm. As discussed above, your enthusiasm will give you energy, and energy is what you will need to confront the challenges ahead of you. You now are starting to understand that to truly find your "why," you most likely are going to have many challenges to face but get excited about that. It is so important to develop your character with enthusiasm. Remember, even the bad times will be great with the right attitude and proper perspective and understanding that you are on a journey. When you understand that the journey is where you learn how to develop your proper character and your love factor. Having an understanding of how to recognize how your "why" will be developed is important. This is very important because when you reach what you might think is a roadblock, it is simply a little challenge that you need to get excited about because it is probably a learning lesson that God wanted you to experience. Many times, as we thought that we were traveling on the right path, God put a roadblock, a challenge in front of us so that we would realize that it was not the right path at all. Remember, failure is not failure; it is time to rejoice. It is building your character! It is simply a closed door. It is time to immediately look for the open door that will lead you on your path for God's plan.

Who Do You Associate With? The Law of Association

Who do you associate with? Who you associate with will play a major role in developing your character and, believe it or not, is the reason that so many do not find their own why in life. They listen to the wrong people. We simply have a lot of negative people in our world. "What makes you think you will become successful?" "You are not smart enough to do that!" "Don't become too big for your britches!" Being a dreamer means that you most likely will take many shots across the bow from your family and friends. You see they do not want you to become successful because it takes away their excuses for being complacent.

Who you associate with, for so many, is the biggest influence on their life, as many people take advice on life from those who have no clue as to what life is really all about. So be careful of who you take advice from.

Decisions: a matter of making the right choices

When we are young, our parents are instrumental in helping us to make the right decisions. As we grow older, our decision-making is a product of our education, actual experiences, common sense, and gut feelings, and being influenced by others. But unfortunately, at times, we make the wrong decisions because we are influenced by people that seem to have your best interest in mind but have no clue what life is really all about. So how are they qualified to give advice? So consequently, many times we make the wrong choices in life.

If you hang out with criminals, you will probably become a criminal.

As our sons were growing up, sometimes we were concerned who they were spending their time with because of the law of association. Our oldest son David, about thirteen, was associating with a few young men that we

WHAT'S LIFE ALL ABOUT?

felt were not going to provide the best influence on him. I sat David down, and we had a conversation talking about the "law of association." I said to him, "As you go through life, you want to choose carefully who you associate with. If you hang out with criminals, you will probably become a criminal." David, of all our sons, was the one that took *my lessons of life speeches* seriously. I cannot tell you over the years how many times David would come back to me with the law of association, and he would tell me, "Well, I had to have the law of association talk with Tim last night. David not only got it. He was an advocate for it and many times would pass on that lesson of life to his friends that might be associating with the wrong people."

As you go through life, look to associate with people that emulate the love factor and look to influence those that are lost and have not found their "why."

> "Do not be misled: 'Bad company corrupts good character'" (1 Cor. 15:33).

Respect

Having and giving respect for others will become an important aspect in developing your character for life. You first must respect yourself; you need to be confident and stand firm on your principles and morals in life and do not be wishy-washy about making decisions. If you are confident, and you display the love factor in your life, you will find that people will give you respect. You will want to give respect to others as well. You may not always agree with their decisions, but you must give them respect for having made them.

When I was growing up and started school, it was still taught that you always gave your parents, your teachers, and elders' automatic respect. We were taught to say, "Yes, ma'am, yes, sir," we would never think to talk back to our parents or a teacher.

> "To speak evil of no one, to avoid quarreling, to be gentle, and to show perfect courtesy toward all people" (Titus 3:2).

If you go through life and you give respect to others as you find your "why" in life, and as you develop your love factor, I believe that you will receive a high degree of respect from those whom you associate with and meet, in your life.

Remember to be humble

As you reach levels of success, or you make achievements, do not stop to read you own press releases. Be humble in all you do and recognize and give credit to God. It is always nice to receive praise but make sure it comes from others and not yourself. Remember that most achievements are achieved with the help of others, and God, so remember to give credit where due.

> A man's pride brings him low, but a man of lowly spirit gains honor. (Prov. 29:23)

> For whoever exalts himself will be humbled, and whoever humbles himself will be exalted. (Matt. 23:12)

> God opposes the proud but gives grace to the humble… Humble yourselves before the Lord and he will lift you up. (James 4:6, 10)

> Do nothing out of selfish ambition or vain conceit, but in humility consider others better than yourselves. Each of you should look not only to your own interests, but also to the interests of others. (Phil. 2:3, 4)

Develop your confidence

In working on your character, building self-confidence is an important factor. One of the most interesting things about confidence is you would think that it would mean to be confident in yourself. That you can do it! This is true to a certain degree, but as you understand God's plan for your life, you will understand that God gives you the confidence to achieve anything because he is the one that will answer your prayers and give you the knowledge, the wisdom, and the understanding to accomplish whatever your vision and dreams end up leading you to do. So be confident in your faith!

Take responsibility for all your actions

You are going to make mistakes, and that is okay! However, take responsibility for all your actions, and if you make a mistake, immediately admit that you made a mistake. Be sure to apologize to those that were offended or hurt in any way by your mistake.

Do not tell lies

It is very important as you develop you character in life…do not lie. It is so hard to trust someone who lies. Telling even a little lie can destroy your integrity and your character.

As our sons were growing up, once in a while we would catch them in a lie, and of course, they would have to have a *lesson-in-life speech* from Dad. The one thing that I told them was that in telling a lie, what ends up happening is that you end up telling another lie to cover yourself from the first lie. Before you know it, it is hard for anyone to believe a word you are saying. It is always better to never lie, so you do not have to worry about what you said or how you said it. It is best to just always tell the truth the first time.

Never stop learning

As you find your passion in life, whether that be in what you are doing for a living or what God has called you to do outside of what you do for a living, be prepared. Study and be knowledgeable. This will give you confidence. When we started Full Circle Energy, I was clueless, especially on the scientific side of this business. So I started to do very extensive research in the field of waste to energy. I studied the terms used. I studied the competition and made a concentrated effort to learn everything I could. After a short period, not only did I know our technology, I could talk the talk, and when talking to engineers, they wanted to know what engineering school I attended. I would tell them that I was not an engineer but completed enough study to have a Hard Knocks PhD. I look forward to learning new things and life is a learning experience every day. Look forward to being prepared.

Whatever you do, never think that you have arrived and that you know it all. Never stop learning, continue to get better, and remember to ask the Lord for knowledge and wisdom. He is all-knowing, and he will lead you to the knowledge you need to develop your knowledge in whatever you do that leads you to your "why" in life.

Do not expect it, earn it!

So many people today just expect a free ride without doing a thing. Our welfare system extends from one generation to the next and has become a way of life for many. The Lord wanted us to be giving and help the poor, but he did not plan for your life to be lazy and expect to be taken care of when you have the capability to work. What does the Lord feel about the lazy people who believe they are entitled to all the benefits of the world yet are not willing to work?

> The sluggard will not plow by reason of the cold; therefore shall he beg in harvest, and have nothing. (Prov. 20:4 KJV)

> For even when we were with you, this we commanded you, that if any would not work, neither should he eat. (2 Thess. 3:10 KJV)

> "You lazy fool, look at an ant. Watch it closely; let it teach you a thing or two. Nobody has to tell it what to do. All summer it stores up food; at harvest it stockpiles provisions. So how long are you going to laze around doing nothing? How long before you get out of bed? A nap here, a nap there, a day off here, a day off there, sit back, take it easy—do you know what comes next? Just this: You can look forward to a dirt-poor life, poverty your permanent houseguest!" (Prov. 6:6 MSG)

God Is the Master Teacher

God is the all-time master teacher, and the Bible is the ultimate source for advice for everyday life. Reading and studying the Scriptures is the very best way to learn from God.

> "Whoever gives heed to instruction prospers, and blessed is he who trusts in the Lord" (Prov. 16:20).

You can learn from criticism. I learned early in life that if someone is criticizing you, do not take offense; simply listen to the lessons that the criticism brings and evaluate it and learn from it. I realize that it is hard to take criticism sometimes but look at it as an opportunity to evaluate a different perspective. It just might be a perspective that you agree with and you might discover some truth.

> "Anyone willing to be corrected is on the pathway to life.
> Anyone refusing has lost his chance" (Prov. 10:17).

Attitude

According to the *Merriam-Webster Dictionary*, the word *attitude* means "an internal position or feeling with regard to something else." Other words often used as synonyms are disposition.

It has been said that your attitude will determine your attitude in life. You have a choice to have a positive attitude or a negative attitude. Making a choice to have a positive attitude is what God wants you to do. Being positive and reflecting happiness in your life will have a positive effect on those you touch in your life.

> "But the fruit of the Spirit is love, joy, peace, patience, kindness, goodness, faithfulness" (Gal. 5:22).

Developing a positive attitude for living your life for many is not an easy task. It is much easier to look for the negatives of life as we are affected by it every day on the news, and in the newspaper. Unfortunately, most people are affected by these influences and negative surroundings. Their attitude that they bring to work most of the time is negative. Do not associate with those that have a negative attitude. That is why it is so important for you to realize that part of your "why" in life is to develop your loving spirit in a positive reflection of life. This will bring optimism and happiness into people's lives. With you having a positive attitude in all you say and do will have a huge impact on those that you work with and associate with. The Lord wants you to live your life "Christ-like."

How would Christ react to a negative situation? It is important for you to be the one at work, at school, in all that you do to be the one that brings optimism and happiness and joy through always expressing your positive attitude. Let it be you that never displays a discouraging word.

Attitude is not so much what happens to you, but how you react to what happens to you. Your reaction in a positive way will encourage and give comfort to those that you associate with in the workplace or in life in general.

The following was taken from the work of Dr. Dale A. Robbins on attitude. This does a great job in discussing the attitude you should have under certain circumstances.

Good Attitudes

According to scripture, your attitude toward life, your circumstances, or toward other people should always be like the Lord's—as is defined by scripture. Good attitudes are generally demonstrated in being positive, encouraging, loving, humble, teachable, cooperative, considerate, selfless, loyal, persevering and so forth (Gal. 5:22–23).

To God—Our attitude should be reverence, submission, love, trust, humbleness, obedience, worshipful, and prayerful. (Psa. 111:10, Mark 12:30, John 14:15, Jas. 4:7, 1 Sam. 15:23)

To God's Children—Our attitude should be love, forgiveness, consideration, caring, encouragement, kindness, humility, unselfishness, respectful, and impartial. (John 13:34–35, 15:12, Rom. 12:10, 13:10, 15:7, Jas. 2:9, Eph. 4:2, 4:32, Col. 3:16, 1 Thes. 5:11, Heb. 3:13, 1 Cor. 13:4–8).

To Authority—Our attitude should be respectful, cooperative, accountable, humble, helpful, encouraging, loyal. Not resentful, defiant or disrespectful. (Heb. 13:17, 1 Pet. 2:13–15)

To Hard Circumstances—Our attitude should be patience, thankfulness, persevering, believing. (Rom. 8:28, Gal. 1:9)

To Our Church—Our attitude should be respectful, faithful, cooperative, helpful, willingness, dependable, participating, encouraging. (1 Cor. 10:32, 1 Cor. 14:12, Heb. 2:12)

To Duty—Our attitude should be faithfulness, responsibleness, obedience, cooperation, endurance. (Luke 16:10, 1 Cor. 4:2)

WHAT'S LIFE ALL ABOUT?

To Unfairness—Our attitude should be patience, humility, confident in God's justice. (Rom. 12:19, Luke 18:7)

To Disappointment or Tragedy—Our attitude should be humility, submission to God, prayerful, confidence in God's fairness. (Psa. 62:5, Jer. 17:5, Deut. 32:4, Job 13:15, Rom. 8:28)

To the Lost—Our attitude should be compassionate, forgiving, encouraging, helpful, reconciling them to God. (2 Cor. 5:18, 2 Pet. 3:9, Matt. 18:11–14)

To Sin—Our attitude should be uncompromising, unaccepting, intolerant, unsympathetic, yet compassionate and reconciliatory for the repentant. (Matt. 18:8–9, Gal. 6:1)

To Success—Our attitude should be humble, grateful, God-glorifying, not self-exalting or forgetful to God. (Jas. 4:6, 10, Prov. 16:18)

To Misunderstanding—Our attitude should be peacemaking, reconciliatory, patient, forgiving. (Col. 3:13, Matt. 5:9, Phil. 2:14)

Avoid Negative Work Attitudes

Being negative at work can create an endless cycle of bad feelings and hurt. If you are the one that brings in the bad negative attitude, understand that you need to be the one to change. Become the shining light, not the bearer of bad news.

The power of words what comes out of your mouth!

"Let no unwholesome word proceed from your mouth, but only such a word as is good for edification according to the need of the moment, that it may give grace to those who hear" (Eph. 4:29).

As we go through life, it is so important to understand that your character is developed and reflected by what comes out of your mouth. What are you saying to people? Remember, in developing your love factor, everything that comes out of your mouth needs to be said with a loving, caring, joyous heart.

We just love to talk negativity in our society. Work on you! When you talk, remember to always look at the positive side of things and express in words the positive. This will set you aside from everyone around you.

People hear all day from everyone regarding the negative of life. They are tired of hearing the negative. If you become the one person in their life that is positive and uplifting, they will want to associate with you and will want to emulate you.

It's not what you say but how you say it!

So many times, it is not what we say, but how we say something that is critical in being positive. When you correct your children for something that they did wrong, how do you say it? Is it with a kind, warm heart, or is it with an angry negative tone? Do you know that from your tone of your voice and the sharpness of your voice that you can say the exact same words but can have totally different meanings? Learn to recognize that how you say words can drastically change the meaning of what you actually said. When you talk, do not have an arrogant, negative attitude in your voice. Talk with a smile in your voice. In correcting your children as you are talking to them, understand how you are presenting the words. Is it in a loving, positive way or a negative angry way? Remember as your children need discipline and do things that are not acceptable to you. As you discipline them, always remember that they, as persons, were not bad, but the actions they did were what was wrong. In other words, you will always love them, but you were not pleased with the actions they did. So many parents rush to tell their children how stupid they are or what an idiot they are. They say these words in an angry, negative tone of voice that can destroy a child's self-image at a young age. As a parent, you need to discipline your children by loving them and being disappointed in their action, not them. The action is what was wrong; yelling at them as you are correcting them using a negative, angry tone will tell them so much about you being positive or negative. You will pass this behavior on to them whether you want to or not. Correct children by always telling them you love them but explaining that their actions are not acceptable. Do this, and your children will have a high degree of respect for you and as they go through life. They will want to make the right decisions as they will be afraid of letting you down because of the high degree of love that you have shown them. They actually will be more afraid of letting you

WHAT'S LIFE ALL ABOUT?

down than anything. This is accomplished by a loving, caring heart, especially in times of disciplining your children.

Always give an extra 10 percent, give way more than is expected

What do I mean "give an extra 10 percent"? As you go through life, always look to give more than is expected of you. Developing this attitude will bring attention to you, and this will also bring rewards. The best way to explain the value of this attitude is to give you a couple of examples.

While in college, I was working as a program director for the Fresno YMCA. I started a program of white-water rafting on the Kings River. There was a section of the river, about ten miles in length, that had about thirty-two rapids. This section really was one of the most exciting white-water rivers in California. This section of the river had no dams above it, and so the river flow was totally based on snowmelt. The river flow could vary from about one thousand cubic feet per second to in excess of over twenty-five thousand cubic feet per second.

I was able to develop a program that attracted people coming from all over California in the first two years. I graduated from Fresno State in 1973 and moved back to Santa Maria, California, to start my first travel agency. The YMCA did not have anyone to run the program that I developed. They were getting many calls from individuals and groups wanting to participate. The YMCA told me that since they had no one to run the program, they asked if I would like to take over the white-water rafting program as a commercial company. I accepted, and we developed the Kings River Expeditions into one of the finest white-water river experiences available. When I sold the company after our 1981 season, we had several thousand people on a waiting list. We ran six days a week and were sold out each year.

How did we develop this white-water experience where we had to turn down business? The key element that we operated on was "*Give our customers way more than they expected.*" We operated a twoday trip with one starting on Friday night and ending on Sunday. Another starting Sunday night, ending on Tuesday. One starting on Wednesday night, ending on Friday. Everyone expected a great ride on the rapids, but what we provided was a total recreational experience. This experience included food that they did not expect, a fantastic campfire program with a jug band, skits, and a river rat induction ceremony. Each participate received a special "river rat shirt." Each year, the shirt was a new color. Once you were inducted into the river rat society, if you came back the second year, you were able to help the staff induct the rookies. Everyone really looked forward to that. Our campfire program was so good that the other two rafting companies would come to see our program.

With our Kings River Expeditions, we developed a philosophy of always providing at least an extra 10 percent effort in everything we did with the program. We did many little things that our customers loved, and it kept them coming back year after year. One of things we did was that you were assigned one river guide for your two-day trip. We found that each customer did not compare one river guide over another because they always had the same river guide. Each river guide took great care of the two couples that were in his or her boat. After we ended our first day on the river, we would have lunch, and then we would take everyone to a special spot on the river called Mill Creek. This was a small stream on the Kings where the water was warm and had small waterfalls to sit under. This provided a little Jacuzzi action along with little water slides. Everyone loved this special spot and made the afternoon a real delight.

Our meals many times were a deep pit where we cooked turkeys, ham and roast underground with baked potatoes, and all the trimmings. After dinner, we put on this special river rat induction ceremony followed by a great campfire program.

In our hiring of staff, we hired college students at Fresno State that were

WHAT'S LIFE ALL ABOUT?

"people" people. We found that our competition hired river guides, and most of them were not people-oriented. Our staff were all hired on their people skills. We took the attitude that if they wanted to be a river guide, we had the confidence to train them in the skills they would need on the river. We did not have time to train them in being a people person. This strategy was fantastic as we had such a talented group of staff. Our customers could not believe that we could hire such talented "all-American" young staff. They were talented as river guides. Cooked fantastic meals, totally catered to their every need, and then put on a campfire program that really was a fantastic show.

We literally blew them away with all the little extras that we did to make their experience so fantastic.

How did we develop such a large waiting list? The marketing approach that we decided to take was to simply go after the group business. We had five trips coming from Santa Clara from the Memorex Corporation, law firms, YMCA groups, Boy Scouts, and we had groups coming from Los Angeles, Santa Maria, the Bay Area, and many parts of California.

When one group finished their trip on the last day, they said they just had the time of their life. We would ask the leader of the group if they wanted to come back next year. Every group said yes, absolutely. We would explain to them that we would save this exact equivalent date for them next year and had them sign a reservation form before they left our camp. We told them that we would send them the confirmation form with deposit requirements in February. So year after year, we would have the same groups booked, and many of the corporations like Memorex wanted to add to their five trips that they already had booked. This happened all because we took the attitude that we were going to give everyone that participated way more than they ever expected. They were blown away by the whole experience. Developing this program over ten years was truly a blessing, but it was not the ultimate plan that God had for my life. However, it was a learning experience that God wanted me to experience for what he had in mind for me in his ultimate plan.

One other story involved our oldest son, David! David is an overachiever in everything he takes on. In high school, he was in the top 25 students in his graduating class of 650. While attending Fresno State, he was heavily involved with his fraternity. He was holding down two jobs, carrying eighteen units while achieving a 3.8 gradepoint average. David has a dream of having his own production company. While he is working to achieve his dream, he has had several jobs in the restaurant and bar business. In Los Angeles, he became the top waiter at a Macaroni Grill. David would show up to work many times at least two hours ahead of when he was to clock in. He went over his section to make sure every chair and table was extra clean.

With all his customers, he overwhelmed them with service. If your drink of water or soda was half empty, he had another one sitting by it. You would never ever have to ask David for more water or drink. David had a knack for knowing what the customer wanted and would provide service before the customer would ask for it. His attitude toward his customers was so positive. It was easy to understand, that's why so many customers would request to be in David's section. He ended up developing regular customers, and his tips ended up providing a very comfortable life as he kept working toward his dream of his production company. David told me that one regular customer ended up paying him close to three thousand dollars a year in just tips. David gave way more than the extra 10 percent. He gave an extra mile to his customers and to each company that he has worked for. One of the keys for David giving that extra 10 percent was that David provided this service using everything that he had learned about the love factor. He smiled; his words were kind and complimentary. Every expression and act were completed with a loving, caring heart. At every company that David has worked for, he became that company's most valuable asset. A caring, loving individual that went way beyond the call of duty to impact people's lives in a positive way. He made each of his customers feel like they were the king or queen for the day.

Our son David and I

WHAT'S LIFE ALL ABOUT?

Whatever you do in life, for work, be sure to set a goal to give that extra 10 percent. This effort tells people that you care, that you are a servant; you want to make a difference. Believe me, the rewards that come back to you will be worth the extra effort. When you make the effort to impact people's lives in a positive way with a caring, loving heart, you will see the benefit.

> Remember this: Whoever sows sparingly will also reap sparingly, and whoever sows generously will also reap generously. Each man should give what he has decided in his heart to give, not reluctantly or under compulsion, for God loves a cheerful giver. And God is able to make all grace abound to you, so that in all things at all times, having all that you need, you will abound in every good work. (2 Cor. 9:6–7)

Most people in their job and in their life do just what is necessary to "*get by.*"

Our son Bryan, out of high school was not sure what he wanted for a career like so many young men just graduating from high school. He started working for In-N-Out Burger and completed their management training program. He was transferred to a location in Phoenix, Arizona, where he stayed for about two years. Bryan has always loved people, but after a few years with In-N-Out Burger, he decided that was not the career he wanted. After coming back to Fresno and staying with us, he decided that he would really like to work in the medical field. Bryan enrolled in an intense schooling program to become a medical technician. He was the only male in his class of twenty-eight. That did not bother him as he was focused on his studies and became the valedictorian of his class, having the best grade-point average of 4.2. Bryan has always understood that in life if you want to succeed, you concentrate on the task at hand. He never missed class; he always did not only what was necessary to pass the class but went way beyond that to be the very best. He always worked hard and stayed focused. Bryan decided one day that he wanted to join a gym and started working out. Well, again, he was focused and two of the trainers at the gym where he worked out who also competed in bodybuilding contests. These two have been doing that for many years and told Bryan that he should enter a bodybuilding contest that was coming up. At first, he was not sure he wanted to do that but decided that he would go ahead and train for it. Well, in his first contest ever, he won his weight division in his class and took second overall in the overall competition. Here are a couple of pictures of Bryan at the contest.

Bryan has always given that extra 10 percent to become the best at whatever he sets his mind to do.

God does not want you to be mediocre!

Make your decisions in your life knowing that God loves you. He wants you to make a positive impact on everyone that your life comes in contact with. Whether that be on the job, in school, in church, or any organizations you join. Make an impact in the service clubs you join, the organizations that you get involved in regarding your children. These might include the PTA or coaching. Decide that you will be the one that will stand out because you were willing to give that extra 10 percent. I have found that the warm, fuzzy feelings come to you when you have this type of attitude. Knowing that your efforts truly made a difference in all you do is worth the extra effort. So you decide to be the go-to person. The person your boss can count on. The person that people look up and respect. They will know that the extra 10 percent that you always give is done in a way that you do not boast about it. You do not expect special treatment back because you are so giving. You do it because it impacts people's lives in such a positive way that it is what God would want you to do as a part of his plan for your life.

Trust

Many people have a hard time trusting other people. Rightfully so, as so many people have shown that they cannot be trustworthy. In my life, especially after understanding how God did have a plan for my life, it was hard to trust most people. It seems like every time you thought you could trust someone, they would let you down. I found that there was only one sure source of trust that I could count on 100 percent of the time and that was the Bible. Knowing and having faith in the Word of God, I knew I could trust and count on it to be the truth.

Many times, as we experience the trials and tribulations of life, we find ourselves in situations that you do not know who to trust or if you can really trust anyone. We can always trust God with a faith and knowing that he will always be there for us.

> "Trust in the Lord with all your heart and lean not on your own understanding; in all your ways acknowledge him and he will make your paths straight" (Prov. 3:5–6).

Many regard the Bible as archaic and irrelevant. If you explore the Bible, you will find time-tested principles that will give you hope and will renew your soul to get excited about life. You need to trust these principles and apply them in your everyday life.

> So that your trust may be in the Lord, I teach you today, even you. (Prov. 22:19)

> A greedy man stirs up dissension, but he who trusts in the Lord will prosper. (Prov. 28:25)

Often, our friends and people that we count on the most sometimes let us down. They have good intentions, but they are human and make mistakes. You will always want to be the person that is trustworthy. Be the person that others can count on. For you, know that you can always count on God. You can place your trust in Him, and you will know that he will never let you down.

> "Fear of man will prove to be a snare, but whoever trusts in the Lord is kept safe" (Prov. 29:25).

7

Be There for Others!

Be there for others and learn to be a friend. Life provides us many opportunities to make friends, yet most people only have a few friends. Why is that? We do not make an effort to become a friend. Making a new friend is really very easy and becomes very rewarding.

> "To speak evil of no one, to avoid quarreling, to be gentle, and to show perfect courtesy toward all people" (Titus 3:2).

I read this statement somewhere but not sure who to give credit to:

> There are four things that you cannot recover!
> The stone after the throw,
> The word after it's said,
> The occasion after it's over,
> The time after it's gone.

Life truly is too short, and that is why you must live each day with gusto. Be careful with the words you say as the right words can be very uplifting for someone, and the wrong words can crush like a stone. By having the true love factor, you will realize that all your words to others need to be uplifting words of encouragement and love.

> "A man that has friends must show himself friendly: and there is a friend that sticks closer than a brother" (Prov. 18:24).

Learn to be a friend. As we go through life, we meet many people, but how many do you cultivate into a friend? Part of your "why" will be cultivating friends. How do you make a new friend? Well, as we have previously discussed, you will want to get involved. You will meet people that are part of the organizations that you join. Once you join, make a point to get to know the members. Ask questions, listen, and show a caring, friendly attitude. Show them that you have an interest in them. Plan on setting times to get together. Invite them over for coffee, for dinner, or plan to meet them at a function. You see, by getting involved and being a joiner, you will have the opportunity to meet many people. Develop the skill to turn those you meet into friends. Everyone has the opportunity to make friends, and yes, it does take some effort. The effort is ten times more rewarding than being the stick-in-the-mud, never seeing anyone, never go anywhere type of person. Get a zest for life…go and get engaged.

The Occasions in Your Life

As you go through life, you are going to have the opportunity to see your son participate in sports. You need to be there. You will have the opportunity to attend your daughter's dance recital; you need to be there. You will have the opportunity to attend a good friend's parent's funeral. You need to be there to support and show your love for that person, even if you did not know the parent. You will have opportunities to be at friend's birthday parties. You need to be there. If you are invited to an occasion, you need to be there. For part of the love factor of life is be supportive to your family, friends, and all you meet.

If you are invited to an occasion, whether that be a wedding, funeral, dance recital, sports event, birthday party, Christmas open house, friends get-together, or whatever the occasion, you need to attend. The fact that you were invited tells you that whoever invited you cares about you and thinks enough of you to want you to be a part of the occasion. Just being there for people is important in showing your loving, caring spirit that you have for life is what life is all about.

When you are there to see your son at that football game and they know that you are there to support them, it builds the loving spirit and the relationship so strong that in the future when they reflect on the past, they

WHAT'S LIFE ALL ABOUT?

will always know that you were always there for them. Being there for others whether family, friends, or acquaintance is part of developing your love factor and what life is all about.

My wife and I have some very special friends going back to the high school years, and we have been vacationing with the family of one of them for many years. During that process, we had become close to his sister and brother-in-law who lived in Bakersfield, 110 miles south of our home. The couple living in Bakersfield have a son Jake who ended up being a very good football player. He ended up calling us Uncle Fred and Aunt Mary. During his high school football games, we would make a point to travel to see Jake play football. Jake was so appreciative that we would travel 110 miles to see him play; it touched him in a very positive way. When Jake went on to play football at Bakersfield Junior College, Mary and I made a point to attend at least three of his games. One of the games, he did not know we were coming, and after the game, we went down on the field to see him and congratulate him on such a great game that he played. He was so touched that we traveled to see him that tears came to him as he gave us a big hug and told us he loved us. He told us he could not believe that we had come to see him. One of our best friends who was Jake's real uncle did not come to see him that year, and we live in the same town. He was too busy to make a trip to see his only nephew.

Jake's sister at the time had a fifteen-month-old boy, which

made Jake his uncle. We overheard Jake telling his mother that whatever his nephew participated in, he was going to be there for him, playing catch, watching his games, or whatever he did. You could feel the disappointment in his voice that his real uncle never came to see him in the big games, but Uncle Fred and Aunt Mary made the special trips to see him.

Going to see Jake play football.

Plan and take the time to attend occasions. Part of life is living day-to-day in giving of yourself, which can make a big difference in affecting other lives in such a positive way. So many people are just living for the destination: When I retire, then I will have time to do things. Once I get that big promotion, then I will make time to attend events. Living their life for the destination and not living along the journey. Life is a day-to-day business, and if you are not being a part of people's lives each day, you are missing what life is all about.

If you have not made a point to be a participant in "all of the occasions" in your family and friends' life, just make that decision that "Starting today, I am going to change. I will be there for everyone. I will be there with a loving, caring, positive attitude, knowing that my presence will make a difference to someone." If you do this with a sincere, loving heart, you will not believe what a warm, fuzzy feeling you will experience. Being there for others in a loving, caring, sincere way will bring tremendous joy to you and to everyone your life touches. It is what life is all about.

Live One Day at a Time

Most people are planning for tomorrow, which makes them not really live until tomorrow arrives. Many people have many regrets about their past, and they are always worrying so much about the future that they do not spend time just enjoying today! You need to make a decision to live each day like it was your last. Have joy in the "now moment."

> "Jesus said, 'Don't be anxious about tomorrow—
> God will take care of your tomorrows. Live one day
> at a time" (Matt. 6:34).

Be a Friend

Being a friend is one of the most important things about growing in your life's work. Look to become a friend wherever you go and what you do. While you spend a good part of your life at work doesn't make sense to make friends with everyone that you see each day? Become a friend with your fellow workers. Take the time to have a caring heart and take the time to learn about their lives and how you can be there for them when needed. If you go to work with great friends, wouldn't that make your job so much more enjoyable? Work on becoming a good friend and become creative in how you can make your job fun. What would motivate anyone to show up

WHAT'S LIFE ALL ABOUT?

to be with people for eight hours of their day and be around people they do not like? You should be the one that becomes a friend to everyone. I know that to become friends with all the people that you work with could present a challenge. If you plan on being in your job for a while, wouldn't it make sense to make the decision that you are going to become a friend to everyone? Just working on your love factor while at work will make a dramatic difference in how people react to you. They will want to become your friend.

The following story is very touching, yet we have probably all known someone like this.

> One day, when I was a freshman in high school, I saw a kid from my class was walking home from school. His name was Kyle.
>
> It looked like he was carrying all of his books.
>
> I thought to myself, *Why would anyone bring home all his books on a Friday? He must really be a nerd.*
>
> I had quite a weekend planned (parties and a football game with my friends tomorrow afternoon), so I shrugged my shoulders and went on. As I was walking, I saw a bunch of kids running toward him. They ran at him, knocking all his books out of his arms and tripping him so he landed in the dirt.
>
> His glasses went flying, and I saw them land in the grass about ten feet from him.
>
> He looked up, and I saw this terrible sadness in his eyes.
>
> My heart went out to him. So I jogged over to him as he crawled around looking for his glasses, and I saw a tear in his eye.
>
> As I handed him his glasses, I said, "Those guys are jerks. They really should get lives."
>
> He looked at me and said, "Hey, thanks!"
>
> There was a big smile on his face. It was one of those smiles that showed real gratitude.
>
> I helped him pick up his books and asked him where he lived.
>
> As it turned out, he lived near me, so I asked him why I had never seen him before. He said he

had gone to private school before now.

I would have never hung out with a private school kid before.

We talked all the way home, and I carried some of his books.

He turned out to be a pretty cool kid. I asked him if he wanted to play a little football with my friends.

He said yes.

We hung out all weekend, and the more I got to know Kyle, the more I liked him, and my friends thought the same of him.

Monday morning came, and there was Kyle with the huge stack of books again.

I stopped him and said, "Boy, you are gonna really build some serious muscles with this pile of books every day!"

He just laughed and handed me half the books.

Over the next four years, Kyle and I became best friends.

When we were seniors, we began to think about college.

Kyle decided on Georgetown, and I was going to Duke.

I knew that we would always be friends, that the miles would never be a problem. He was going to be a doctor, and I was going for business on a football scholarship.

Kyle was valedictorian of our class.

I teased him all the time about being a nerd.

He had to prepare a speech for graduation.

I was so glad it wasn't me having to get up there and speak.

On graduation day, I saw Kyle. He looked great.

He was one of those guys that really found himself during high school.

He filled out and actually looked good in glasses.

WHAT'S LIFE ALL ABOUT?

He had more dates than I had and all the girls loved him.

Boy, sometimes I was jealous! Today was one of those days.

I could see that he was nervous about his speech.

So smacked him on the back and said, "Hey, big guy, you'll be great!"

He looked at me with one of those looks (the really grateful one) and smiled.

"Thanks," he said.

As he started his speech, he cleared his throat, and began, "Graduation is a time to thank those who helped you make it through those tough years. Your parents, your teachers, your siblings, maybe a coach…but mostly your friends…I am here to tell all of you that being a friend to someone is the best gift you can give them. I am going to tell you a story."

I just looked at my friend with disbelief as he told the first day we met.

He had planned to kill himself over the weekend.

He talked of how he had cleaned out his locker so his mom wouldn't have to do it later and was carrying his stuff home.

He looked hard at me and gave me a little smile.

"Thankfully, I was saved. My friend saved me from doing the unspeakable."

I heard the gasp go through the crowd as this handsome, popular boy told us all about his weakest moment.

I saw his mom and dad looking at me and smiling that same grateful smile.

Not until that moment did I realize its depth.

Never underestimate the power of your actions.

With one small gesture, you can change a person's life.

> For better or for worse.
> God puts us all in each other's lives to impact one another in some way.

I remember someone like this in high school. Most of us made fun of him; he was the school nerd. Being involved with our high school reunions I made a special effort to try and locate Dennis but was unsuccessful. I felt that I needed to talk to him and find out how his life turned out and really wanted to apologize for how he was treated in high school. We can be so cruel to people sometimes, and if we really knew how we hurt people with just our words and actions toward them, we would think before we act.

> "Whoever brings blessing will be enriched, and one who waters will himself be watered" (Prov. 11:25).

8

Learn to Do All the Little Things Well!

As we go through life, we can affect people's lives wherever we go. I have found so many times it is the little things that you can do that can have a big impact on influencing people's lives in a positive way.

Giving Someone a Call

As you meet people in your life and you may have even become friends, over time, we tend to lose those friends because either they moved away, or the friendship just was neglected because there was no contact. Make a point to call someone to tell them you were thinking about them every day. Friends are such a valuable asset toward your life purpose. Nurture all your friends like they were flowers in your garden, and you do not want them to die. You water them, you pick out the weeds, you watch over them. Do the same with all your friends and the people you meet so they will also become a friend.

If you have family members that live out of town or even in another state from where you live, then you need to give them a call on a regular basis. Your parents you should give a call to each week. Brothers and sisters, you should call at least a couple times a month. Other relatives, be sure to call them on their birthday and on special holidays to wish them a warm greeting.

> "Dear children, let us not love with words or tongue
> but with actions and in truth" (1 John 3:18 NIV).

Make a list of all the friends that you have not contacted in a year or more. Sit down and give them a call to tell them that you were thinking about them and wanted to touch base to see what was happening in their lives. Keep in contact and be there for them. A friend is like a very precious stone; keep them polished and hold them close because they are way too valuable to lose.

Sending Cards

Cultivating friends! When you meet someone, be sure to get their business card if they have one. Write down their contact information, and then send them a short little note telling them how much you enjoyed the opportunity to meet them. As you develop a friendship, write down their birthdays, their anniversaries. Keep them where you will be able to send them a birthday or anniversary card. Give them a call to wish them happy birthday or happy anniversary. This will make their day that you remembered these happy times in their life.

Our pastor G. L. Johnson and his wife Jackie Johnson were such special people, and we loved them so much. Jackie is one that sends out many cards. Mary and I were always getting a card from her and our pastor. She always sent a card for all the holidays, Thanksgiving card, Christmas card, and a Fourth of July card. However, most of the cards were just cards to say we wanted you to know how special you are and how they cherish our friendship. We were not the only one that received these cards, just about everyone in our church had received cards from them. It truly is a special talent that means so much to others and represents an extension of your love.

Sending a warm card tells the person receiving it that you care, and that you are sending them love. Sending cards sincerely is such a great way to nurture a friendship.

Sending holiday cards: keep adding to your Christmas card list and send out Christmas cards. At work, you should send everyone you work with a Christmas card. During the course of the year, get to know your mailman, your UPS delivery person, your FedEx delivery person, and all the people that you do business with. Send everyone a card. Express your appreciation for the service they provide. This is an expression that lets them know that you care and that you appreciate them.

So many times in life, it is all the little things that you can do to make a positive impact in someone's life that will be a part of your "why" in life. The Lord loves you so very much. He wants you to love all those you come in contact with. There really are so many ways to express love to others. I have put my thoughts together in this book, and it has been a huge reminder to me that I need to start being a better loving person and make changes in my life to get better at loving people. I know that God in developing your plan for your life wants you to develop your love factor toward people. God wants you to become a loving, caring person so you would become the person that would make a difference in people's lives. So no matter how you move forward to discover God's plan for your life, always work on you to develop your character to become a loving, caring person. Because this will always be a part of His plan for you!

Do not fight it; the rewards of becoming a giver and developing a loving spirit to effect people in a positive way are so great. Just decide to go with it! Start making changes in your habits, in your actions, in your attitude to become the loving, caring soul that God intended you to be.

The Importance of Communication

In your day-to-day communication, give thanks. Give thanks to everyone you work with. Let the janitor know how appreciative you are of the good work he does. Let the secretaries know how much you appreciate their hard work. Always communicate how thankful you are and appreciative you are to be working with such great people. Be the one to always communicate to everyone you work with, in a positive, caring, and loving attitude. You will soon notice how positive your work environment will become. You will see how coworkers will treat you.

You should always be the first one to acknowledge a job well done. You need to be the one person at your work, in your home, and in all your associations to acknowledge the effort that someone has made to do the job well. If you make the effort to have this type of attitude, soon everyone you meet will just be excited to see you coming into the room.

You should always be the one that makes a point to celebrate and be appreciative with special occasions. Celebrate at work, at home, and whatever group you have associations with. Make sure that you celebrate birthdays, holidays, and anniversaries. Find things to celebrate and appreciate people. Celebrate the length of time on the job, their first year, five years, ten years, etc., days in a row without a sick day or days at the workplace without an accident. Find things to appreciate people for and then celebrate. "Have fun."

When you communicate, you will always want to be enthusiastic! Your enthusiasm in the workplace, at home, or wherever you go is so infectious.

So always communicate with enthusiasm. Be sure to smile, have fun, and let people you work with know that it is important, no matter what you are doing, to have fun. So many in the workplace do not understand that if your employees are having fun, they will enjoy their job. They will not be thinking all the time how they wish they could quit. If you are the one that makes that extra effort to make things fun, others will want to be around you. They will look to follow you in their actions and attitude. You can be the one that can make a difference.

Be the one that is always doing the extra things from your heart! Be kind, and each day make an effort to be the one everyone can count on. If someone in the office needs a day off to watch their son play in a football game, be the one to cover for them. Be the one to volunteer if someone is needed to plan a birthday party for a coworker. Always be aware of things that you can do to make a positive difference at work and in your home.

Always be the one to look for opportunities to have fun. The one person that is always looking for ways to make things fun is the person that everyone enjoys being around. Let that person be you. Look for ways to have fun even if the tasks you do seem boring.

While I was in junior college in 1967, I was not sure what I wanted to do in life and ended up joining the Navy. At that time, the Navy had what they called the one-two-three program. It required going to reserve meetings for one year, and then two years on active duty, and then three more years in the navy reserves. Since I was not serious about school at that time and did not keep my grades up, I lost my college deferment. I was about to be drafted into the army. Well, the Vietnam War was going on at the time, and I really was not too excited about being in the army. I joined the navy's one-twothree program. While I was attending the first year in navy reserves, attending meetings once a week, I ended up working for the Southern Counties Gas Company. My job was working on a three-man crew fixing broken gas pipes. Mostly it was at residences, and sometimes it was a commercial gas line. One of the crew bosses was old Clarence.

Clarence was about a couple of years away from retiring and was impossible to work with. He was so bad that everyone refused to work with him. He was just cranky, and no matter what you did or how you did it, it was wrong. He would yell at you and tell you what you were doing wrong. What ended up being so funny is that he would tell you one time how to do it, and so you did it that way the next time, and he would yell at you that you were doing it wrong again. It did not matter what you did; it was wrong, and he

WHAT'S LIFE ALL ABOUT?

was going to let you know about it. I decided that I was not going to let this guy get to me. The other crew member I was working with while we were working with Clarence decided to make a game out of his crankiness and just have fun. So before old Clarence would open his mouth, we would guess with each other what he was going to say. It really got to be fun, but we never really let Clarence know what we were doing. We were always respectful and decided that we would just try to overwhelm Clarence with kindness. It got be that we really looked forward to working with him as we knew what to expect, and we had fun, and it helped to have the time go by faster. After a while, Clarence actually became tolerable and after about three months we came to actually respect him, and he learned to give us back respect as well. Clarence was just mad about life and wanted to retire. He just had a negative attitude about everything and everyone. We just decided that we were not going to let him get our goat. I once heard someone say, "If someone is trying to get you goat, just never let him know where you have it tied up."

I tell you this story because the result of this experience was overwhelming. I got called into the corporate office one day. Three of the top management wanted to talk to me. They started off by asking me how have I been able to work for the last six months with Clarence, and we have not had one complaint filed by me about Clarence. They proceeded to explain that nobody had been able to work with Clarence for more than a week before they would inform us there is no way that they can work with him. If they have to work with him, then they will have to quit.

"You have been working with him for six months and not one complaint. How were you able to do that?" I just explained to the management that I could tell that old Clarence just had a bad attitude about life and people and just refused to let his attitude bring mine down.

The management knew that I was going to be leaving for my two years of active duty with the Navy the next month. They proceeded to tell me that when I got out of the Navy that they wanted me to come back to Southern Counties Gas Company. They told me that they were willing to pay for my entire college education and wanted to train me for their upper management for the company. I was flattered but knew I would have to move to the Los Angeles area to live and did not really want to live day-to-day with such a traffic problem. One of the keys in life, no matter what you do or who you work with, is to have fun. Communicate enthusiasm, always be complimentary, develop that love factor in your life. Always have a positive effect on those you meet. You are going to work with those that are lost in life like old Clarence, become their friend, overwhelm them with kindness, and give them respect. They will come around, and you just might become the one person that gave them enough love and respect to have made a major impact in their life.

9

What Are You Worrying About?

> Give all your worries and cares to God, for he cares about you.
>
> —1 Peter 5:7 (NLT)

So many people today are worrying... They are worrying about everything. In school, they worry about getting a good grade, being popular, being able to graduate. People worry about their job, about paying their bills, about their children, about getting a promotion. They worry about what people will think of them. They worry about getting to work on time. They worry about if they are overdressed or underdressed. Parents worry about their children when they hear a cry in the night. We worry about global warming, about driving our car in traffic, about our children driving in traffic. We worry about our educational system, and we worry about our government. We worry about our enemies, about crime, about AIDS, about how to afford to send our kids to college. We worry about drugs and its effect on our society. We worry about medical insurance, about having clean water, about having clean air to breath. We worry about our country moving away from the Christian principles.

> "Don't worry about anything; instead, pray about everything. Tell God what you need, and thank him for all he has done" (Phil. 4:6).

When I was in the third grade and eight years old, I had a bleeding ulcer from worrying. My father was a carpenter, and we moved three times during my third-grade year, and at the last school that I attended, my teacher had everyone in the class to get up in front of the whole class and read out loud their homework or part of the lesson for that day. It scared me to death. I was not a very good reader and was probably toward the low end of our class in reading ability. I worried about it so much that I actually had a bleeding ulcer at eight years of age. I had to take special antiacid medicine three times a day. But I remember my grandmother sat me down and shared some great wisdom with me that I never forgot. She said, "Fred, there are two types of things that you can worry about as you go through life. You can worry about things that you have no control over. If there is absolutely nothing that you can do to change it or do about it, then there is no sense to worry about it." She went on to say the other things that people worry about are things that they can do something about. They can make changes; they can correct what is wrong. They can take action that can correct the thing or things that they are worrying about. If that is the case as you go through life, then you need to take the action to make the changes. Do this and you will not have to worry any longer.

So understanding what my grandmother was telling me is that there is never anything that you should really worry about. Once I accepted the Lord as my savior and realized that the Lord was really like a partner in life, I learned to not worry about anything because I turn my worries over to the Lord.

> "Have I not commanded you? Be strong and courageous. Do not be terrified; do not be discouraged, for the Lord your God will be with you wherever you go" (Josh. 1:9).

If you are worried about something, remember how God protected you and provided for you in the past. Remember God's faithfulness in your life in the past as it will always give you confidence and faith that he will provide for you now. This is a great way to combat worry.

> "Give all your worries and cares to God, for he cares about you" (1 Peter 5:7 NLT).

As we go through life, we often really do worry about everything. I have found and believe that worry is a lack of faith.

WHAT'S LIFE ALL ABOUT?

If you truly believe in your God and believe that he has a plan for your life, he will not put you in harm's way. Go through life with a strong conviction of your faith. If something does go wrong, it was only because God needed you to experience that as a learning lesson for the bigger picture he has for you in the future. So get excited about your troubles and do not worry. We have put so much stress on ourselves for no reason.

> "I sought the Lord, and he answered me; he
> delivered me from all my fears" (Ps. 34:4).

J mentioned earlier that at the age of eight, I was terrified of getting up in front of people to talk or read. What I learned from this experience is that I learned to overcome what I was afraid of. I have spoken in front of thousands of people, and I love it today. It is so exciting to be able to be in front of thousands of people and share. To be able to give back and hopefully make a positive impact in people's lives.

Once you accept the Lord into your life and you study his Word, you will develop the understanding and the true joy of life itself. Worrying then seems so odd because you know that God has a plan for your life and usually what people worry about are related around other people, not God. Do not worry about anything that would cause you to worry if it is related to someone else. If you truly understand this, you will have a knowing that you know that you know and worrying seems a little silly.

> "Commit your way unto the Lord; trust also in
> Him; and He shall bring it to pass" (Ps. 37:5).

Do not worry about the past, as you need to focus your thoughts on your future. It is important to leave your past in the past. You cannot go back and change it. The only thing that you can change is your attitude to move forward in the future with a positive, loving, caring heart for your future. So stop worrying about something you either did or did not do in the past. Ask the Lord to forgive your past sins and get excited about what he has in store for your future.

Think about what most people worry about. Most worries are worrying about other people. Your boss, a deadline someone has placed on you, and many times, just little things that do not add up to anything when you understand the big picture of life. Those things are not what life is really all about.

If you understand that God does have a plan for your life and you need not worry about it or anything, for it shows your lack of faith.

> "So, my dear brothers and sisters, be strong and steady, always enthusiastic about the Lord's work, for you know that nothing you do for the Lord is ever useless" (1 Cor. 15:58).

People spend so much of their life worrying they do not take time to really understand life or enjoy life. They are so busy worrying about a bear that might be in the forest that they missed the unbelievable creation of God's work found in the forest. Those fantastic big trees, the birds, that bubbling brook, the fresh smell of the wildflowers blooming on a spring day. Stop worrying and start thanking the Lord for such a wonderful life.

Pray about the things you are tempted to worry about. Let your requests be made known to God with thanksgiving.

If you are a worrier, I suggest that you take out a piece of paper and write down all the things large and small in life that you are thankful for.

Are you thankful for your warm home, that you have running water in it? That you have a toilet in it? That you have heat and air-conditioning in your home? Are you thankful that you have electricity, a washer and dryer, a refrigerator, a stove, an oven, a microwave, a shower with hot water, a car to drive? Are your thankful for your family, for your friends, for the freedom you have, for the opportunities you have? Are you thankful that you have the opportunity to have a grocery store? Are you thankful for the many stores in your community that have just about anything you need or would ever desire to eat? We take for granted so many little things to be thankful for that most of the population of the world do not have. The next time you are in a grocery store, look around and see all the choices you have. Then think about being in the middle of Africa and what type of grocery store do you think they have.

Continue to make the list out of all the things you are thankful for. Are you thankful for your job, your parents, your classmates, your spouse, your schooling, your church, your opportunities to serve others? Are you thankful for your country, our servicemen and women, your city's policemen and women, firemen and women? Are you thankful for all the recreational opportunities you have? Walking on the beach, riding your bike in the park? Are your thankful to be able to go waterskiing, snow skiing, going to a football, basketball, baseball, soccer game, or many of the other sporting events that we have an opportunity to enjoy? Are you thankful that you have a phone, a television, a computer, a fax machine? Are you thankful that

WHAT'S LIFE ALL ABOUT?

you can attend any movie you wish to see? Are you thankful that all of your garbage is picked up for you at your house every week? You know that your list could go on and on and on…

But now, after you have completed this list, what are you worried about? Call upon the Lord because he provides all the things you just listed that you are thankful for. Give him a chance for you to be thankful to him for the things you are worrying about. Turn them over to the Lord if you cannot do anything about the worry. If you can do something to change or eliminate your worry…do it! So you will not have to worry about it any longer. If you are not able to make the change or do not have the power to make the change, then give it to the Lord as nothing is too large for him to handle. It is just that simple. Move through your life with faith, hope, and with your eyes always open, looking for what the Lord will do in your life. He will bring joy, happiness, and always keep your purpose into perspective. If you have not invited the Lord into your life, many of the things that I discuss in this book will become very hard. You will keep running into walls, and what life is all about could pass you by. I hope that you will not let that happen. Asking the Lord to come into your life is like having the best partner, the best friend, the all-knowing, all-caring protector as your partner in life. That is what the Lord wants to be. He loves you and cares about you. You are one of his children, and like most good, loving parents, there is nothing they would not do for their child. They will protect them even with their life if it came down to that. They will do everything they can to pass on wisdom and knowledge. They will help to develop their child to be a loving and caring person. They will do anything to provide for their child, to nurture them and protect them. That is what God wants to do for you.

You see, God does not force his will on you. You need to accept God as your creator and savior and accept that he has such a wonderful plan for your life. Where most people go wrong is that they do not believe it. Even many Christians do not believe it as they still worry, and many Christians are not on God's plan for their life. They are on their own plan and that is why they worry; they are depressed and lost. They are just putting in their time and missing the true joy of life. I hope that if you are reading this, you understand that if you feel lost, unloved, depressed, and do not know what to do, I hope that you will seek the Lord as your savior first and then start to dream. Stop your worrying and start to get excited about life for all the happiness and joy it brings.

Just thinking about how wonderful life is, I just get goose bumps all over.

Write down your list of all the things you are thankful for in your life. Write down all the obvious things, but also all the little things that most people just take for granted. Whenever you start to worry about anything or are feeling down, go to this list and read over it and get excited about your life.

When we put Matthew 6 and Philippians 4 together, we find God saying He will supply all our needs—emotional needs, physical needs, spiritual needs, relational needs—if we trust Him. God says, *"You don't have to worry. It's unnecessary. I'll take care of you."*

Christians will trust God with their eternal salvation, yet they will not trust God with their family, business, or personal problems! It really comes down to the question, "Do I have faith, or do I worry about it?" I think you know the right path to choose.

> Put your trust in who God is. Remind yourself of His love, wisdom, power to guide, protect and provide. Do you believe He is who He says? Renew your mind by dwelling on these things instead of your worries. (Phil. 4:8)

> For God hath not given us the spirit of fear; but of power, and of love, and of a sound mind. (2 Tim. 1:7)

Knowing God has a plan for your life, you need to trust his plan and stop worrying! Move from this day forward with excitement about just turning all your worries over to the Lord.

10

Is Your Job Your "Why"? A Plan to Move Forward

> "For I know the plans I have for you," says the Lord. "They are plans for good and not for evil, to give you a future and a hope... You will find me when you seek me.
>
> —Jeremiah 29:11, 13

Where are you in your life in regard to what you do that pays your bills? Do you believe that your job is your real why in life and is pleasing to the Lord? Does your job provide you the opportunity to serve the Lord in a way that you are able to serve people?

Do you enjoy what you do on the job, or do you feel that you are just putting in your time enduring it because it pays the bills? If you had all the money you needed to pay your bills, would you stay on your job?

I ask these questions because so many people are miserable at the job they are doing. They put in eight hours a day or forty hours per week, a good part of their life in misery. They do not know how to get out of the rut they are in. They do not like what they do, or the people they work with and feel like their life does not have much meaning.

We will want to explore how to make the positive changes in your life regarding "your job!"

> "A man's heart plans his way, but the Lord directs his steps" (Prov. 16:9).

"A man's heart plans his way, but the Lord directs his steps." Wow, what is the Lord telling you? I believe that God's plan for your life will direct you to be able to make your living by doing something that is a joy to your heart; in other words, do something that you like doing. Do not stay in a job that does not make you happy. Life is way too short for you to spend a lifetime in a career doing something that you are not happy doing.

> For I know the thoughts that I think toward you, says the Lord, thoughts of peace and not of evil, to give you a future and a hope. (Jer. 29:11)

> Commit thy works unto the Lord, and thy thoughts shall be established. (Prov. 16:3)

What do these scriptures mean? They simply mean that if you commit your life to the Lord, he will provide you with the right thoughts, dreams, and vision to move you in the right direction. This is very hard for many people to accept or believe, but I need to tell you trust in the Lord with all your heart. Why is life so hard for so many? They have lost their faith in the Lord. It is time for people to come to an understanding as to why they were born and who created them. Do you really think that the Lord would create you in his own image and then not lead you to a joyous life and just throw you to the wolves? If you are tired of being sick and tired, then commit your life to the Lord; have a new beginning for your life. I cannot begin to tell you how wonderful life can be. It will give you such hope and joy that you really were born for a reason. You will get excited about the journey of your life and wake up every morning with such gratitude in your heart. That is the way it is supposed to be.

> "The steps of a good man are ordered by the Lord" (Ps. 37:23).

What does this verse mean? It means that you need to take the first step in changing your life. Start to dream and start to plan to take a step in a new direction. Work on your dream as you work on a plan to make the career changes that will lead you in the right direction. God will be there to take your hand and help you to make the right decisions. Before you know it, you will know that you are in the right place doing the right things that will make your day-to-day life filled with joy and happiness. You will know that you are on the right path and the plan that God wants and had planned for your life.

> "The intelligent man is always open to new ideas. In fact, he looks for them" (Prov. 18:15).

Many Christians find their life in one turmoil after another and wonder why. The reason is that they do not listen to God; they do not have the faith that God truly has a plan for their life, and they attempt to do it on their own. This might be you! Why are you fighting it?

> "Trust in the Lord with all your heart and lean not on your own understanding; in all your ways acknowledge Him, and He shall direct your paths" (Prov. 3:5).

Become a Visionary

The Spirit of God is to focus on others. Without vision, most people become self-centered. Are you living in the vision and purpose for your life?

Pray…be happy right where you are. Remain positive no matter the circumstances and how they will dictate how you will respond. Always have a positive attitude. Most people are intimidated by their circumstances. Our fulfillment is not determined by our circumstances. Allow yourself to be in a pit and give thanks for being there. This will give you perspective, and you will know that you cannot do it yourself as you need to know that the Lord is the reason.

You will be tested so remain faithful and never lose your faith. Learn to be content no matter the circumstances. How do you deal with despair? Are you filled with hope? The Lord is always with you. Look in each day for happiness, not in some distant time frame. Well, when I get a new home, I will be happy. When I retire, I will be happy. When I get that new job, I will be happy. No, be happy every hour of every day.

The job that you currently have might be the right place for you and is what God had planned for you, but maybe you have not accepted that fact that you need to make some changes in your life. Where are you right now, and how do you treat people and your fellow workers? Maybe the thing that is missing is your loving, caring spirit that comes with you developing the love factor in your life.

Do not be resentful; be thankful. You will be tempted to love material things, a new car, a big home, and expensive clothes. Do not be tempted by these material things. Let me make this very clear; it is okay to have nice things, but do not let those be your driving force for your life.

You will be tempted to worship personal status. To become someone that is recognized to have status in your city. Once again, it is okay to be recognized and to become a person of stature but humble yourself and never let becoming a person of stature be your driving force in your life. Be a servant to others.

Always remember it is not where you start but how you finish. If you absolutely knew that when you were born that the Lord had a very distinct plan for your life, but it is not always clear what that plan is, you need to understand that it starts with dreaming. And the dream develops into a strong vision. Also keep in mind that your dreams and vision should not be all self-motivated. How is your dream and vision going to help mankind? The Lord will give you vision, and he will give you dreams that will lead you to your purpose. If you understand this, then you will be excited to move in a direction that your dreams and vision take you. God will put on your heart a calling that will truly make you happy. As you have these feel- ings or gut feelings, they just might be God telling you something. Act on them!

> Scripture tells us, "Sometimes it takes a painful
> situation to make us change our ways" (Prov. 20:30).

You need to know that you are going to be tested. Your faith and hope will be tested over and over, but knowing this ahead of time, it is important to be happy about it. Be joyous for all the challenges that are put in front of you. I personally believe that the more challenges you have, the greater the victory that the Lord has planned for your life. So as you go through life, get excited about the challenges and maintain a strong, positive attitude of hope and faith.

You need to have an attitude that your lows are going to be much higher than most people's highs. Developing this strong positive attitude is a commitment to your faith. Have your hope is in the plan that the Lord has for your life and it will be revealed to you. The Lord loves you as he loves everyone. You will develop a very special spot in his heart if you maintain your hope and faith. There is nothing he cannot do in your life.

WHAT'S LIFE ALL ABOUT?

> I will instruct you and teach you in the way
> should go; I will guide you with My eye. (Ps. 32:8)

> The Lord will guide you continually. (Isa. 58:11)

It should be very clear to you that these verses clearly outline God's job is to direct you in every step in this life. If you have God directing your every step, what are you worried about? Cast all your burdens upon the Lord. He will take care of you and give you direction to get back on the right path. Why do so many people including Christians believe that they can make better choices for their life than what the Lord has planned for them?

> "To enjoy your work and to accept your lot in
> life—that indeed is a gift from God" (Eccles. 5:19).

This is what Solomon, the King of Israel, and the author of Proverbs observed.

One of the motivations to write this book was to hopefully reach someone that would understand that the Lord does have a plan for your life. You do not have to have a mundane life of worry, unhappiness, and living form one crisis to other. The Lord can set you free and will direct you to the life that was planned for you since you were born. You need to accept the Lord and accept the fact that his plan for your life is one of joy and fantastic happiness. You also need to accept that your life up until now might just be the right path because he wanted you to learn many valuable lessons. Accept that reading this book might have been a spark that was ignited in you to realize that you needed to make some changes. You need to get on your right path. God is waiting for you. He is excited for you. He loves you. He has such joy and happiness to bring to you. You just need to accept him and then ask for his help. You see, he gives you complete freedom of choice. You do not have to accept him, and you do not have to experience the great plan he had planned for you. God will let you go on your own path, but why would you ever want to do that?

I know how many of you feel. You either have not accepted the Lord into your life, or if you have, you really are not sure about this whole "*God has a plan for my life*" thing. Believe me, I understand. I was there. I have always been an entrepreneur with what I thought was a very positive attitude regarding life. I finally realized after many trials that I could not do it on my own. Something was missing in my life. I was a very hard worker. I was positive. I was excited about life, but there was something missing. I could not put my finger on it. I eventually realized it was not having the Lord in my camp. I did not grow up in typical Christian home where we went to church; however, I believe that my parents, especially my mother, was more spiritual than most "Christians." She taught us the "golden rule": Do unto others as you would have them do unto you. Not man's new golden rule: "*He who has the gold makes the rules.*" Even though my mother was not the typical Christian, she instilled into my sister and I Christian principles for how to live our life in treating people with a caring, loving spirit in our attitude about life. To work hard in no matter what task you took on. Do things right and be respectful of people.

There are probably many of you that can relate to this type of up bringing. Even when I was led to the Lord and accepted Jesus Christ as my Lord and Savior, I did not truly understand the true meaning of life in what it really meant to have a relationship with the Lord.

By this, I mean to trust him with all your burdens and turning your life over to him. Understanding that my life was not mine, it was his that he gave me to live a "Christ-like" life. I started to study his word from the Bible, but it was not until I was over fifty years of age and my path led me into the renewable energy industry when I begin to totally turn my life over to him. I realized then that everything that I had experienced in life was a training ground for his true purpose for my life. You see so many of you right now that are reading this have experienced many things in your life. But you probably have not really felt that you have led a "Christ-like life" and you have probably felt like you have been in a whirlwind, wondering what you are going to do when you grow up. Well, that is how I felt, and then one day in church, our pastor was speaking on understanding that the Lord has a plan for your life, and you need to trust him first. Then ask him to lead you to it and that everything happens for a reason. Wow, a light went on! I knew that I was now finally on my right plan, the plan that the Lord had arranged for me before I was born. It was so exciting, as I could look back on all my failures and successes, my ups and downs, and on my relationships with people and where the Lord was taking me, and I got so excited I could not sleep.

> "If you abide in me, and my words abide in you,
> you shall ask what you will, and it shall be done
> unto you" (John 15:7).

Every scripture I read—I can say yes, I can relate to that! Yes, the Lord is right on. He does have a plan! He will lead you on the right path. He loves and cares for you and will not lead you in the wrong direction. Yes, if you totally move forward with complete faith, yes! Yes! Yes! I got it… I finally got it.

I hope that you will take the steps necessary to start on your true path in life. Knowing what we have shared in this work, believe it can happen for you! Act on becoming the best you can be. Start your new path by working on you and becoming that loving spirit by working every day on your personal love factor traits. This is the best way to begin your "new life!"

> Delight yourself also in the Lord, and He shall give you the desires of your heart. Commit your way to the Lord, trust also in Him, and He shall bring it to pass… Rest in the Lord, and wait patiently for Him. (Ps. 37:4, 7)

> And I say to you, "Ask, and it shall be given unto you, seek, and you shall find, knock, and it shall be opened to you." (Luke 11:9)

Once you understand that you were created by God for a purpose in which God had planned for you your life. Then for you to not act on that life would not make much sense. Trying to find what life is all about on your own does not make much sense either. I pray that you will decide to have faith in the Lord and that you start on your journey to find your why. Get excited about the challenges you will face. Enjoy every day and take joy in what comes your way. Ask the Lord in prayer each day for direction, for knowledge, and for wisdom. Know that he will not let you down so always move forward with faith no matter how hard you think the road is. God will build your character, study his Word, and live your life with purpose in serving others.

> "For I know the plans I have for you," says the Lord. "They are plans for good and not for evil, to give you a future and a hope…You will find me when you seek me, if you look for me in earnest" (Jer. 29:11, 13).

The end.

But I pray a new beginning for you!

ENDORSEMENTS

Hi, Fred,

Thank you again for your wonderful, inspired, and powerful book! I just finished it and my dream and vision has been lifted and so is my spirit of faith. Thank you for sharing so much from your experiences, challenges, and life. I really love all the scriptures, which I plan to refresh in my memory again and memorize so I can just say them out loud as I walk. Awesome job.
"Life is so spectacular when you are on God's plan!"
by Dr. Laurie Roth

Fred YOUR book, is POWERFUL. I could visualize your excitement as you wrote, animation, gestures, and facial expressions and all. Maybe you can do a video presentation of your book someday, or at least a lecture series.

This book needs to be distributed throughout the business world, Fred. The whole world would benefit by reading it and putting its tenets into practice. There are thousands out there that do not know you, but who need to read what you say in your book.

Fred, I have just recently been inspired to pursue my own dreams. Part of that inspiration was YOUR BOOK. God has been after me to get off my duff and go where He leads, but your book was a confirmation and a kick in the tail.

I pray that the Lord blesses you and Mary. And I pray that He blesses your book so that it rises to the Best Seller list. We need Godly guidance today more than ever.

Bixby Calderwood

If you want real success, achievement in your family, work, and life, and to get off the treadmill of "almost and failure" you need to put the coffee on, sit down, and read this book. Open your heart a little, and this inspired work will change your life. I have known Fred Furrow for many years and seen firsthand through his many trials and struggles his choice to stay with perseverance and faith in the Lord Jesus when things were falling apart around him, money was scarce, and he couldn't see a thing. He just trusted in God, prayed some more, and waited in faith. God showed up again and again. He resisted over and over throughout his life the seduction and temptation to jump off the faith and power train back into regret, insecurity, discouragement, and fear. I know Fred and he is the real deal, humble to the core, and with wisdom from God that he shares in his down-to-earth style, warmth, realness, and impact. The one thing I know about Fred Furrow is he does not do boring, selfish, and waste of time in any part of his life. Read this and come alive and then rock your world. That is what I did, and my dreams are bigger than ever. Look out, world.

Commentator, host, producer, writer, survivor, and mom

Fred Furrow's book, *What Is Life All About?* is an inspiration to help you to recognize your purpose in life. God has a perfect plan for everyone. If you are having problems in your life, this book just might help you to get back on track to better understand your purpose in life. Through this book, you will come to understand that God gives everyone a road map to discover your purpose in life. I would recommend that everyone read this book to help you find your own why.

Nora Henderson

Fred Furrow has put into printed form what you would expect to gain from an excellent personal mentor. Regardless of your age or situation, you will benefit from Mr. Furrows insight and experience.

Pastor Gene Sperling

My friend Fred Furrow has a beautiful heart. He has helped many people through rough times in their life. With this book, he has brought the word and joy of the Lord to all who read his book.

His presentation using scripture how to live your life brings such meaning and understanding into our lives in a most beneficial way. I would recommend that everyone read this very inspiring book. People that are somewhat confused about life in reading this book can find a very positive perspective in making changes in their own life. *What life is all About* is a must read.

Randye Low

FRED FURROW RECOGNIZED FOR ENTREPRENEURIAL SUCCESS

With over four decades of expertise in business ownership to his credit, Mr. Furrow aspires to make a positive impact on the world

On March 21, 2022, Fred Furrow has been included in Marquis Who's Who at Clovis, California. As in all Marquis Who's Who biographical volumes, individuals profiled are selected on the basis of current reference value. Factors such as position, noteworthy accomplishments, visibility, and prominence in a field are all taken into account during the selection process.

Having long harbored a passion for entrepreneurship, Mr. Furrow has developed over a dozen corporations throughout the course of his career. With his businesses, he has aimed to make a positive difference in the lives of others.

Mr. Furrow currently works as the founder and chairman of Remarkable Technologies Inc. and as the cofounder and president of Full Circle Energy Inc.

Mr. Furrow's companies implement waste-to-energy technologies and systems for the production of renewable fuels or power generation without yielding any pollution. Remarkable Technologies Inc. boasts an array of technologies specializing in water and energy, as well as in food production, health, housing, transportation, and other industries that promote the well-being and growth of humanity. Mr. Furrow holds a Bachelor of Science in Business Administration from California State University, Fresno. Looking toward the future, he is in the process of publishing his book, What Life Is All About. Outside of his primary vocational pursuits of the development of humanitarian projects worldwide, Mr. Furrow plans on devoting much of his time to his Extended Hands of Christ Foundation.

About Marquis Who's Who

Since 1899, when A. N. Marquis printed the First Edition of Who's Who in America, Marquis Who's Who has chronicled the lives of the most accomplished individuals and innovators from every significant field of endeavor, including politics, business, medicine, law, education, art, religion, and entertainment. Today, Who's Who in America remains an essential biographical source for thousands of researchers, journalists, librarians, and executive search firms around the world. Marquis publications may be visited at the official Marquis Who's Who website at www.marquiswhoswho.com.

Fred and Mia Furrow

Fred and Mia Furrow and their five boys

ABOUT THE AUTHOR

Fred Furrow Recognized for Entrepreneurial Success

The author, Fred Furrow

With over four decades of expertise in business ownership to his credit, Mr. Furrow aspires to make a positive impact on the world.

Having long harbored a passion for entrepreneurship, Mr. Furrow has developed over a dozen corporations throughout the course of his career. With his businesses, he has aimed to make a positive difference in the lives of others.

Mr. Furrow's companies boast an array of technologies specializing in water and energy, as well as in food production, healthcare, housing, transportation, and other industries that promote the well-being and growth of humanity.

FRED FURROW

Mr. Furrow holds a Bachelor of Science in Business Administration from California State University. Outside of his primary vocational pursuits of the development of humanitarian projects worldwide, Mr. Furrow plans on devoting much of his time to his extended hands of Christ Foundation. Mr. Furrow's passion is making an impact in other people's lives and believes that this is *what life is all about!*

Clovis, California—January 18, 2022, Fred Furrow has been included in Marquis Who's Who. As in all Marquis Who's Who biographical volumes, individuals profiled are selected on the basis of current refence value. Factors such as positions, noteworthy accomplishments, visibility, and prominence in a field are all considered during the selection process.

www.ingramcontent.com/pod-product-compliance
Lightning Source LLC
Chambersburg PA
CBHW020504030426
42337CB00011B/230